# The Flip Side

## 64 Point-of-View Monologs for Teens

# HEATHER H. HENDERSON

MERIWETHER PUBLISHING LTD.
Colorado Springs, Colorado

**Meriwether Publishing Ltd., Publisher**
P.O. Box 7710
Colorado Springs, CO 80933

**Editor: Theodore O. Zapel**
**Typesetting: Elisabeth Hendricks**
**Cover design: Janice Melvin**

**Library of Congress Cataloging-in-Publication Data**

Henderson, Heather, 1970-
        The flip side : 64 point-of-view monologs for teens / Heather Henderson.
-- 1st ed.
            p.        cm.
        ISBN 1-56608-045-2 (pbk.)
        1. Monologues. 2. Acting--Auditions.        I. Title.
    PN2080.H46      1998
    812'.54--dc21                                                                98-29298
                                                                                      CIP

2    3    4    5    6    7    8        03    02    01    00    99

# Contents

# Preface

"Ms. Henderson, Josh hit Me!"
"I did not. She hit me first!"

After working with middle school students for five years, I've learned that no matter who started it, both kids will think they're right. Instead of trying to mediate, I went back to my desk and wrote the argument down. Thus, *The Flip Side* was born...

*The Flip Side* is a unique collection of monologs that give student actors a chance to do what they like best: argue! If lawyers have made a career out of finding the opposing argument then middle schoolers have made it an art form! Though all the monologs may not be in direct contrast to each other, they do offer an alternate view on a similar situation. Students should have no trouble finding a topic that they can identify with. For instance, your class jock may have fun presenting "Jungle Gym Fever," a monolog on the joys of P. E., while another student may relate to "P.U. or P. E. Stinks!" The monologs are best presented as a pair so your class can see the difference in the two points of view. The monologs are also a good way for those particularly hard-headed kids to see what it's like to walk a mile in another's shoes.

When my Advanced Drama class, The Stargazers, presented *The Flip Side* to our school, the curtain opened to a stage full of students all placed back-to-back. Some students stood, some were sitting in chairs or on the floor, but the idea of being placed back-to-back helped the actors communicate to the audience that the opinions were in contrast to each other. It should go without saying that there are a multitude of other staging options as well. Props in *The Flip Side* are minimal and most can be mimed. Remember that the lines are not written in stone. If something doesn't feel natural, change it! Most importantly, have fun with the monologs. Arguing doesn't always have to be a negative thing.

By the way, I never did figure out who hit whom first...

Heather H. Henderson

1

NOTE: The numerals running vertically down the left margin of each page of dialog are for the convenience of the director. With these, he/she may easily direct attention to a specific passage.

# Ladies...

# The Really Stupid Idea

1      I told her it was a really stupid idea, but did she listen to
2  me? No! I told her we would get in trouble and be grounded
3  for the rest of our lives (or worse!), but did she listen to me?
4  Of course not. I told her that I didn't want to be a part of it,
5  and she did it anyway. Some friend she turned out to be.
6      See, we were just messing around in Wal-Mart trying on
7  clothes and stuff. They had the cutest mini-dress in the whole
8  world. I could just picture myself walking down the hall to my
9  locker. I casually lean over to twirl my combination, and Chad
10  sees me. He stops, he stares, he can't believe his eyes. I'm daz-
11  zling, I say hi and smile. He drops to his knees and pledges his
12  undying love for me. He begs me to let him do my bidding. I
13  agree, and we live happily ever after. But I was broke. I had
14  just spent my last ten dollars on the newest "Great Guys" CD.
15  No dough, no dress. I put it back on the rack.
16      *(Shannon's voice Off-stage)* "You're not gonna get it? But
17  you'd look so hot! Chad would flip."
18      "Look," I told her, "even if I took the CD back, I wouldn't
19  have enough. Besides, my mom would kill me." But did she lis-
20  ten to reason? Common sense? Simple math? Nope. Then she
21  proposes this really stupid idea.
22      *(Shannon's voice Off-stage)* "Hey, just put it on and walk
23  out. You could leave your stuff in the dressing room so it would
24  be like a trade."
25      Yeah. Right. Like anyone would believe that I would wear
26  a dress like that to Wal-Mart.
27      *(Shannon's voice Off-stage)* "Dana Johnson does it all the
28  time. You should see the clothes she gets away with. Lots of
29  people do it."
30      All I could think of were the lemmings we learned about in

1    science swan diving off a high cliff to certain death. That
2    and cattle being led to slaughter. This idea had "danger"
3    written all over it.
4        *(Shannon's voice Off-stage)* "Fine. I'll do it for you.
5    Think of it as an early birthday present."
6        I felt sick. I thought I was going to throw up. I ran to the
7    bathroom. My stomach felt as if I had swallowed a porcu-
8    pine. I splashed some water on my face. I tried to convince
9    my reflection that Shannon really wouldn't do something
10   like that. That she was only kidding. The porcupine kept
11   doing somersaults. I knew Shannon was serious. When I got
12   back to the dressing room, I found Shannon's T-shirt and
13   shorts lying on a chair in cubicle #1. Shannon wasn't in
14   them. I heard the store alarm go off. Instead of rushing to
15   Shannon's defense, I closed the door and cried. I told her it
16   was a stupid idea.
17
18
19
20
21
22
23
24
25
26
27
28
29
30
31
32
33
34
35

# Five-Finger Discount

1    *(Talking fast and nervous)* **Look, sir, you've got to believe**
2    **me. This is all a misunderstanding. Really, when my friend**
3    **gets here she'll explain it to you.**
4    *(Aside to audience)* **Come on, Michelle. Where are you?**
5    **    See, she went to the bathroom, well, ran to the bathroom**
6    **'cause she felt sick. I was trying on this dress at the time, and**
7    **I knew I couldn't leave the dressing area and anyway, when**
8    **I'm sick I like to be alone so I figured she might want to be**
9    **alone so I stayed where I was.**
10   *(Aside)* **Michelle, If you don't show up in five seconds, I'm**
11   **gonna kill you. I did this for you.**
12   **    Well, she was gone a really long time, and I started to get**
13   **worried. After all, how long does it take to cough up your**
14   **lunch? But then I thought, maybe she fainted and hit her head**
15   **and was lying on the bathroom floor bleeding to death, and**
16   **I'm still standing around wearing this dress 'cause I wanted to**
17   **show it to her. So I went to the bathroom to look for her** *(Aside)*
18   **(I can't believe you're not going to show up and bail me out.)**
19   **When she wasn't in the bathroom, I went back to the dressing**
20   **room 'cause I figured maybe I missed her on the way in. Well,**
21   **she wasn't there, either. Then I got really worried. Maybe she**
22   **was delirious or had amnesia from hitting her head when she**
23   **fainted and was stumbling around Wal-Mart not knowing who**
24   **she was? Why didn't I page her? Um...er...well, I didn't think**
25   **she would recognize her name with amnesia and all.**
26   *(Aside)* **Remember when I lied for you to Mr. Spaulding?**
27   **You switched the Sex Ed tapes with the "Life of a Butterfly,"**
28   **but I took the blame 'cause it would keep you off the princi-**
29   **pal's list and I never stood a chance anyway.**
30   **    After a few more minutes went by I thought maybe she**

1    went outside to wait for her mom to pick us up. When I'm
2    sick I know I like to have my mom around so that's where I
3    was going, sir, when I set off the alarm. I'm very concerned
4    about my friend. Have you seen her? *(Aside)* I can't believe
5    you let me down. Some kinda friend you turned out to be...
6       Ya know, it's a sign of true friendship when you rush to
7    the aid of a friend without even considering that you could
8    be stopped for shoplifting, don't you think?
9
10
11
12
13
14
15
16
17
18
19
20
21
22
23
24
25
26
27
28
29
30
31
32
33
34
35

# Mirror, Mirror

1    *(Looking in mirror)* **Everyone hates me because I'm beauti-**
2    **ful. No, really. It's true. You should hear the way all the girls**
3    **talk behind my back. Even those that say that they're my**
4    **friends. Oh sure, they're really nice to my face. They save me**
5    **seats at lunch and tell me all the best gossip but it's only**
6    **because they're hoping that when they use my lipstick, Lus-**
7    **cious Berry, it will somehow look as incredible on them as it**
8    **does on me.** *(Gets out compact and lipstick and applies some.)*
9    **See what I mean?** *(Checks reflection in compact.)* **My older sis-**
10   **ter used it once but her boyfriend told her she looked like she**
11   **smeared her face with cherry pie. He didn't say that to me**
12   **though. My sister's jealous of me, too. Boys come over all the**
13   **time to see me, not her. Mom takes me to have my nails done,**
14   **not her. Who's had people stop her on the street and ask if**
15   **she's a model? I'll give you a hint — it's not her! Once I tried**
16   **to help her by telling her that if she combed that ratty-looking**
17   **mane of hers and plucked that shag carpet between her eyes,**
18   **she might stand a chance. Did she thank me? No! In fact, the**
19   **ingrate called me names that I'm not allowed to repeat and**
20   **slammed the door to our room in my face.**
21   **Being beautiful does have its down side. It takes work, ya**
22   **know. I have to get up every day at five in order to look pre-**
23   **sentable for school. Do you think the other girls have to do**
24   **this? No way! They could sleep in until seven-thirty and still be**
25   **ready for the bus by eight 'cause all the preparation in the**
26   **world wouldn't help them. Me, on the other hand, if I forgot**
27   **my mascara just one time in my life, the whole school day**
28   **would come to a screeching halt. All the girls would write me**
29   **notes telling me that I looked tired or to find out if I was feel-**
30   **ing OK and none of the boys would tell me that I had gorgeous**

1   eyes. Then the teachers would get mad because no one was
2   paying attention to them and things would get downright
3   ugly, so to speak. Another bad part about being so attrac-
4   tive is the attention that I get from the teachers. I've seen
5   Mr. Matthews stare at me when he thinks I'm not looking
6   and then when I turn and smile at him, he looks down and
7   blushes. And he's married! It gives all those so-called
8   friends of mine just one more reason to be jealous. He just
9   looks at them like they're little kids. On the other hand,
10   Mrs. Presley always yells at me to pay attention to her.
11   Why? She's such an ugly old bat. I can't stand to look at
12   her. She's got this big, fleshy wart-thing hanging off her
13   cheek. It makes me sick just to look at it. You'd think she'd
14   like someone as pretty as me in her class. It's too bad that
15   beauty can't rub off on a person; she could use some.
16      Sometimes it's so hard to be me, but when faced with
17   the alternative, I definitely wouldn't want to be anyone else.
18   *(Goes back to looking in compact at self.)*
19
20
21
22
23
24
25
26
27
28
29
30
31
32
33
34
35

# Princess Pizzaface

1     My name is Doreen, but hardly anybody ever calls me
2 that. My parents call me "Princess" or "Peanut," but that's
3 better than what the kids at school call me: Pizzaface. Some-
4 times even Puswad. It wasn't always this way. I used to be just
5 like everyone else. Until puberty, that is.
6     I remember my first zit. Right here by my nose. My mom
7 was so proud. "Look, our Princess is growing up!" Yuck, how
8 could she think that this shiny whitehead was a good thing?
9 "Now don't pick it, Doreen, or you'll only make it worse." Boy,
10 isn't that the truth. Once you pick it, the skin around it swells
11 up and gets all red and hot. You might as well have a big, flash-
12 ing, neon sign above your head that reads, "World's Biggest
13 Pimple. Come One, Come All!" And then it multiplies. The
14 first morning, it's just one. The next day you wake up and
15 there's one on your forehead, your chin, your cheekbone.
16 Exxon calls you about an oil slick. The day after that, it's
17 pizza. By the time I got to this stage, I couldn't remember what
18 I used to look like. Jenny McKay told me that lemon juice was
19 a natural astringent and it would clear me right up. Have you
20 ever gotten lemon juice in an open cut? They don't call it cit-
21 ric ACID for nothing! Needless to say it didn't clear me up.
22 Not lemon juice, not baking soda scrubs or oatmeal masks.
23 Not OxyClean pads or Benezoyl Peroxide. Nothing. I thought
24 I was destined to live life in a paper bag.
25     But get this! Tomorrow, I'm going to a dermatologist.
26 That's a doctor who only takes care of skin problems. There's
27 this great new drug that you can only get through a doctor and
28 it's called Accutane. It's so powerful that if you're a girl, you
29 have to be on birth control pills if you've already gotten your
30 period or else it's supposed to give you three-headed babies or

1    something. Not that any boy would want to be seen with me,
2    but just in case. It's the law…Anyway, it's supposed to
3    really work. I'm so excited. I can't imagine not having to play
4    connect the dots on my face. Bye, bye, Princess Pizzaface!
5
6
7
8
9
10
11
12
13
14
15
16
17
18
19
20
21
22
23
24
25
26
27
28
29
30
31
32
33
34
35

# Martha Philips Is a Thief

1　　　Martha Philips is the biggest lying, cheating, two-timing
2　slutty thief I know! She thinks she's so popular simply because
3　her dad is the coach of the football team and all the boys are
4　always over at her house. Does she really think the guys are
5　over there to see her? News flash, Martha, they are there to see
6　Coach Philips, not cheerleader Philips!
7　　　Today was the last straw. There's this new guy, Jeremy
8　Fisher. He just moved here from Florida and he's *sooo* fine.
9　His hair is all bleached out and he's really tan from going to
10　the beach and surfing and whatever else they do in Florida.
11　Anyway, he's the best thing that has happened to this stuck-
12　up, snobby school since the roof to the gym fell in last year
13　under all that snow. We didn't have PE for two months! We
14　didn't have to dress out in freezing weather in that damp,
15　smelly locker room. *(Musing to self)* I wonder how many col-
16　lective prayers were answered that day?
17　　　Oh yeah, Jeremy. So Jeremy moves here, right, and he is
18　*sooo* nice. He talks to everyone and has friends in all the dif-
19　ferent groups. The tough talkers like him 'cause he beat up
20　Tommy Adkins for calling him a fairy. The real athletic guys
21　like him 'cause boy, can he run. They all pick him when
22　they're playing soccer or football. He's smart, he listens to all
23　kinds of music, he fits in everywhere! Well, the first day he was
24　in, like, all of my classes and since he needed someone to show
25　him around, Mr. Roberts asked me. It turned out that he
26　moved in four houses down from me, so I said the next morn-
27　ing we could walk to the bus stop together. He thought that
28　was a great idea. After that we would hang out at lunch and
29　walk home together after school, and a couple of times he even
30　came over to play video games. We, like, became really good

1  friends and all until the other day.
2       Yesterday, I saved a seat for him at lunch like I always
3  do. It's the day the cafeteria makes real pizza instead of the
4  institutional spaghetti-sauce-on-a-slab-of-cardboard kind
5  they usually serve, so it was real crowded. Well, I waited
6  and waited, and finally Mr. Daniels, who supervises our
7  lunch period, said I couldn't save a seat any longer. I ended
8  up eating lunch next to these real nerds who just discovered
9  they could blow bubbles in their milk if they stuck straws
10  up their noses. It was really gross. After school, Jeremy didn't
11  get on the bus either. I got worried. Maybe he was sick and
12  went home with some deadly disease and was lying on the
13  couch suffering, waiting for a friendly face before he took
14  his final breath. When I got to his house, his mom said to
15  come right in, and Jeremy was in the living room watching
16  TV. He was on the couch, all right, with one arm around
17  Martha Philips and he was taking his last breath straight
18  from her lip gloss-covered lips. And I'm sure she wasn't giv-
19  ing him CPR. Jeremy looked really surprised, but Martha
20  just smiled that evil, two-timing smile and snuggled up to
21  Jeremy. It's not fair. I found him first!
22
23
24
25
26
27
28
29
30
31
32
33
34
35

# He Loves Me, He Loves Me Not...

1    (*Picking petals off a flower*) He loves me, he loves me not.
2    He loves me, he loves me not. He loves me! I knew it! Maria
3    Gordon can say anything she wants, but I have the proof right
4    here. He loves me, not her.

5        She's always been jealous of me. Last year when Jeff Turn-
6    er liked me and not her, Maria started spreading these really
7    bad rumors like I went all the way with him and I would with
8    any guy if the price was right. I'm so sure! I didn't even want
9    Jeff Turner to send me those dorky love notes, let alone get
10   that close to me! He liked me, not the other way around.

11       And Randy Taylor. Oh my God, Randy Taylor is just
12   about the finest hunk of man this side of a Chippendale's cal-
13   endar. One night, after our Pop Warner football game, I said,
14   "Good game, Randy" and he said, "Thanks" and smiled the
15   most adorable smile at me. Well, Maria is a cheerleader too, ya
16   know, and she was sort of standing close to me and she thought
17   he smiled at her. As if that could happen! I had to set the
18   record straight and all, but she insists that he still smiled in her
19   direction. Whose smile doesn't go in her direction when her
20   hips are as wide as the Grand Canyon? I'm, like, positively
21   anorexic compared to her.

22       Oh, and I almost forgot about Valentine's Day. She made
23   the biggest fool out of herself. Everybody still talks about it at
24   lunchtime. See, Mrs. Brockman made us compose an original
25   poem for somebody for Valentine's Day. It could be a friend or
26   enemy, even. And then we put them in this big cardboard box
27   all decorated with hearts and doily things. On Valentine's Day,
28   you went up and picked your Valentine out and read it to the
29   class. Well, Joey Allen wrote this poem to me 'cause we were,
30   like, secretly going out. It said:

|    |                                                         |
|----|---------------------------------------------------------|
| 1  | Your hair glistens in the sun.                          |
| 2  | I love to watch the way you run.                        |
| 3  | Your joyful cheer fills me with pride.                  |
| 4  | I cannot keep my love inside.                           |
| 5  | Your laugh is sweet, your eyes are bright.              |
| 6  | I want to hold you in the cold, dark night.             |
| 7  | Say you'll love me to the end.                          |
| 8  | Or can we at least always be friends?                   |
| 9  |                                                         |
| 10 | Isn't that sweet? When he got done reading he was like  |
| 11 | all red, but he's pretty cute so it only made him cuter. Maria |
| 12 | says out loud, "Oh, that's so nice, Joey. Why didn't you tell |
| 13 | me sooner that you like me?" He was like, "Huh? I meant |
| 14 | Martha." Maria got like ten shades darker than Joey, she |
| 15 | was so embarrassed. Can you believe her?                |
| 16 | So today is the last straw. Jeremy Fisher likes me best, |
| 17 | not her, and if she tries any more of her attention-stealing |
| 18 | crap, I'll pick all the petals off a whole bouquet of flowers |
| 19 | to show her who's the fairest one of all!               |
| 20 |                                                         |
| 21 |                                                         |
| 22 |                                                         |
| 23 |                                                         |
| 24 |                                                         |
| 25 |                                                         |
| 26 |                                                         |
| 27 |                                                         |
| 28 |                                                         |
| 29 |                                                         |
| 30 |                                                         |
| 31 |                                                         |
| 32 |                                                         |
| 33 |                                                         |
| 34 |                                                         |
| 35 |                                                         |

# I Love Mrs. Smith

1    *(Runs On-stage, visibly excited.)* **Oh wow!** You're never
2    gonna believe who I have for English: Mrs. Smith! Can you
3    imagine? What luck! Last year I had Mr. Driscoll and he was
4    the worst. He talked really low so we could hardly hear him
5    except when he passed back our tests, then he'd be so mad that
6    he'd scream at us. If he had talked that loud the whole time
7    maybe we would've learned something. Jeez!
8    My sister told me that Mrs. Smith is the best teacher in the
9    whole school. She always decorates her room in these bright
10    colors and changes her bulletin boards a lot so the room is
11    always interesting. I hate teachers who leave up the same stuff
12    all year long and by the time they take it down in June, it's all
13    faded and dusty. Not Mrs. Smith. She puts up a Christmas tree
14    at Christmas and on Halloween she has a real carved pump-
15    kin on her desk that she keeps lit all day. My sister had her
16    seventh period last year and told me that the room smelled like
17    burnt pumpkin, but she gave them candy like a trick-or-treat
18    thing. Can you believe it? A teacher who actually gives the kids
19    candy? And Halloween is just about the best holiday of all. My
20    old homeroom teacher, Mrs. Burchfield, said Halloween was
21    evil and shouldn't be celebrated in school. She's weird. I didn't
22    like her anyway.
23    And Mrs. Smith doesn't use the textbook the way most
24    teachers do. She skips around and only makes the kids read
25    the good parts. She also has this cape that she wears when
26    she's teaching grammar lessons and she calls herself "Gram-
27    mar Girl." Isn't that the coolest? I think I might like to learn
28    about commas and stuff if I got to wear a cape. I know I'm
29    gonna love English this year…
30    What? Oh my God, tell me that you're lying! You're not?

1    Mrs. Smith moved this summer? Where? Canada? What's
2    she doing there? Oh, this is so unfair. Who's the new Eng-
3    lish teacher? Mr. Driscoll? Again? My career as Grammar
4    Girl is over before it's even started! Rats, and I look great
5    in red...
6
7
8
9
10
11
12
13
14
15
16
17
18
19
20
21
22
23
24
25
26
27
28
29
30
31
32
33
34
35

# Mrs. Spit

1     *(Walks slowly On-stage, obviously disgusted.)* **Oh wow.**
2     You're not gonna believe who I have for English next year:
3     Mrs. Smith...Mrs. Spit! Can you imagine? I may be sick. Last
4     year I had Mr. Driscoll. He was so cool! He always stayed real
5     calm even when the kids got all rowdy and loud. He said he
6     wasn't gonna try to be heard above the chaos. He'd just stand
7     there with his arms crossed and eventually everyone would
8     settle down. Then he'd just pick up where he left off. The only
9     time he'd yell at us would be when we really screwed up on a
10    test. But then he only yelled 'cause he cared.
11    My brother told me Mrs. Spit was one of the worst teach-
12    ers in the whole school. She makes a big deal out of the
13    holidays and decorates like a tacky discount store. Every nook
14    and cranny of the classroom has some shiny, metallic star or
15    tissue paper Valentine on it. There isn't a place to rest your
16    eyes except your own desk and who wants to look there? He
17    warned me that at Halloween, she keeps a lighted pumpkin on
18    her desk. Can you imagine what her room smells like at the
19    end of the day? Cooked pumpkin makes me sick! But the
20    worst thing about Mrs. Smith is this habit of hers. You can't
21    sit safely in the front row without a raincoat and an umbrella.
22    She's not called Mrs. Spit for nothing, you know! She gets so
23    excited about whatever she's teaching that little drops of spit
24    start flying around. My brother said that while they were
25    reading "A Christmas Carol" around Christmas, she got so
26    worked up over the scene where Marley tells Scrooge that he'll
27    be visited by three ghosts that a big drop of spit landed on his
28    textbook. He had to go to the clinic.
29    Mr. Driscoll never got ruffled. He was really steady. We
30    worked straight through the textbook so by the time we got to

1     June, we felt like we had really accomplished something.
2     Mrs. Spit jumps all around and you never know where you
3     are. And get this, she wears a cape. Is this very dignified for
4     a grown woman with grandchildren? Like nouns and verbs
5     warrant the excitement for wearing a cape anyway. I'm
6     dreading English this year...
7        What? Oh my God, tell me you're not lying! You're
8     not? Mrs. Spit moved to Canada this summer? That's
9     unbelievable. What great luck! This is excellent. Who's the
10    new teacher? Mr. Driscoll? This is better than winning the
11    lottery! So long, Nanook. I hope your spit doesn't freeze!
12
13
14
15
16
17
18
19
20
21
22
23
24
25
26
27
28
29
30
31
32
33
34
35

# The Sick (of School) Day

1      Every once in a while, my mom lets me take a sick day —
2  a sick of school day, that is. Really! Don't get me wrong, Mom
3  still thinks that I should be in school getting a good education
4  and all, but she understands that a little break can also be just
5  as beneficial.
6      On my sick of school days, I get up and tell Mom that I
7  don't fell like going to school. She always asks me if I have any
8  tests that day. If I say yes, I have to go, so I usually say no even
9  if I really do. I can always make it up in study hall. Then Mom
10  calls the school and says that "Julie isn't feeling well and won't
11  be in today" line. And that's that. It's that easy. After that the
12  day is mine. Mom will usually leave me a list of chores or
13  errands to do, but hey, who am I to complain about emptying
14  the dishwasher when I could be suffering through yet another
15  lab on cell division with my creepy lab partner, Dwayne, who
16  has the worst body odor this side of the garbage dump!
17      Sometimes, Mom takes the day off too and then we have a
18  "Mother/Daughter Day Off." Most of the time we go to Ashton
19  Park which is in a really ritzy section of town. We window shop
20  and go in stores that we could never afford to shop in regularly.
21  We always manage to find something little to splurge on so we
22  can leave the store with one of their bags. Mom calls it "pre-
23  tending to be one of the beautiful people." My favorite place to
24  eat lunch in Ashton Park is called Le Petite Bistro. You eat out-
25  side under this canopy of vines at these cute, little tables only
26  big enough for two people. They serve these amazing omelets
27  that you can get any time of the day. It's really a choice restau-
28  rant. Mom agrees that our mother/daughter days can be just
29  as educational as school. She always makes me figure out the
30  tip in my head or calculate the sales tax on one of our beauti-

1    ful people purchases. Sometimes she gets a little carried
2    away and gives me spelling tests off the menu. If I get one
3    hundred percent, then I get dessert. If not, no chocolate
4    mousse pie for me. These little quizzes are a small price to
5    pay for special time alone with Mom.
6       As a matter of fact, I think I'm beginning to come down
7    with something. Uh-oh. *(Puts hand to forehead to take tem-*
8    *perature.)* It feels like schoolitis again. Good thing there's no
9    cure. *(Calls Off-stage.)* Mom. Hey, Mom! I don't feel so good
10   today... No, I don't have any tests... I think I need to go to
11   the doctor...in Ashton Park. *(Winks at the audience and*
12   *shrugs.)* It's worth a shot!
13
14
15
16
17
18
19
20
21
22
23
24
25
26
27
28
29
30
31
32
33
34
35

# Camping Out

1     Of all the places that I am forced to go, school is the worst.
2  I hate to go to church because it's so boring but I go anyway
3  'cause my mom likes the whole family to do stuff together on
4  the weekends. Besides, it's only an hour. I hate to go see my
5  grandmother who's in a nursing home 'cause it's all so
6  depressing and creepy. All these old people are just sitting
7  around waiting to die. And it smells — like death and pee. The
8  worst part about that visit is my grandmother is so out of it she
9  never knows who I am, but I go anyway, and it's only once a
10  month. School is, like, every day of your life from the time you
11  can walk, talk and go to the bathroom by yourself until you're
12  old enough to move out. By that time, you're too old to have
13  any real fun! And school is for hours and hours too. Just think
14  of all the stuff you could do if you didn't have to go to school.
15  I get depressed thinking about it…
16     Last month, I came up with a new plan. I figured, hey, they
17  can force me to go to school but they can't make me go to class.
18  I hang out in the girl's bathroom most of the time. It's not the
19  nicest place in the world, but at least there I get to do what I
20  want. I bring my backpack full of stuff to keep me busy. I lis-
21  ten to 106.8 on my headset. I bring my TeenGirl magazines
22  from home. I even brought this cross-stitch project that I
23  started when I was ten but never finished. Sometimes it gets
24  boring but then I think about what we'd be doing in class and
25  I always find some way to pass the time.
26     The best part about camping out is that there are always
27  people coming and going. You would not believe the people I
28  have met since I'm no longer confined to just one team. This
29  girl, Leslie, comes in at the same time every day and we share
30  a cigarette. She says she really admires what I'm doing, but if

1    she gets caught skipping school one more time, her mother
2    is, like, gonna send her away to boarding school or some-
3    thing. And then there's this girl, Toni. She said her sister,
4    who is in high school, knows this girl who holds the record
5    for cutting classes in school — three whole months worth!
6    It's hard to believe that I used to be scared of the truant
7    officer when I was in elementary school. He's probably
8    something like the Boogey Man, an idea parents tell their
9    kids to keep them in line. Our school is so overcrowded that
10   I'm sure my teachers are glad that I don't show.
11       Lately, I've been having problems avoiding our campus
12   advisors. Advisors, ha! Cops is more like it. I think this girl,
13   Kathy, on my team, saw me when I was in the library the
14   other day. She came in to return a book and I thought I cov-
15   ered my face with the magazine in time, but I guess not. She
16   probably told our teachers who told our principal, who told
17   the campus cops to watch out for me. Now every time some-
18   one comes into the bathroom, I have to run for an open
19   stall. Camping out isn't as much fun as it used to be. In fact,
20   it's made me so jumpy that even when I'm home, I can't
21   relax. Still, at least I'm not in that jail called class. I'm my
22   own free woman, sort of.
23
24
25
26
27
28
29
30
31
32
33
34
35

# It's Lonely at the Top

1     Everybody expects your life to be great if you're popular,
2    but it's not. Everyone expects you to always be perfect and
3    never have any problems or get upset or have a bad day when
4    you're popular, but I'm telling you, it just doesn't work out
5    that way. Some of us popular people have bad lifetimes. The
6    sad thing is that nobody notices 'cause they're so busy being
7    impressed with who you are. As far as I'm concerned, I've had
8    it. I don't want to be popular anymore. For just one day, I'd
9    love to be somebody normal.
10    I've been popular my whole life. Honest, I was in a maga-
11   zine ad when I was a baby. I've been doing TV commercials
12   since I was three, and last year I was the cover model for Teen-
13   Girl magazine's "Bright New Star of the Year." You should've
14   seen the big deal they made about me at school. It's not like I
15   saved somebody's life or invented a machine or discovered the
16   cure for cancer. I just smiled for a camera.
17    My parents are too busy making me famous to really act
18   like parents. They are always arranging another photo shoot
19   or scheduling an interview. My dad even quit his regular job
20   to be my agent. "Our baby's gonna make us a fortune," he
21   says. Just once I wish they'd ask me if I want to be somebody's
22   fortune.
23    At school, it's not any better. My teachers are all extra nice
24   to me, not 'cause I'm smart, which I am, but because they
25   want me to remember them when I'm rich and famous. At this
26   rate, by the time I leave high school, I'll have to remember
27   about fifty-five different teachers. I could go out with any guy
28   I want but the only reason they want to go out with me is
29   because they could then say they've gone out with me. This one
30   guy, Marco, is some sort of a hero because he's actually been

1   my boyfriend. I broke up with him when I heard he was
2   bragging that he made it with me. It didn't happen, but all
3   the guys believed him anyway. In their own small, imma-
4   ture minds they can't imagine someone who looks good
5   enough to be on the cover of a magazine might actually be
6   a decent person inside and be saving herself for the one guy
7   who loves her for her mind, not her body.
8       The girls at school are just as bad. They pretend to be
9   nice to my face, but I've heard some of the things they say
10  when I'm not around. They only want me around so they
11  can say I'm one of their very best friends. They ask me to
12  come over and want to borrow my clothes and gossip about
13  the boys in our classes, but I don't think that any of them
14  really care that I'd rather be a scientist than a size two.
15  They just hope that some of my popularity wears off on
16  them which it usually does.
17      There's this one girl, Doreen. Everybody calls her Piz-
18  zaface 'cause she has this very bad acne problem. The truth
19  is, I really admire her. She's strong and independent and
20  everyone pretty much leaves her alone. All the teachers like
21  her because she's smart, not because she looks good. I'm
22  sure her parents love her for who she is, not because she's a
23  potential superstar. One time I asked her to be my lab part-
24  ner in a science class instead of asking one of the girls who
25  usually follows me around. The class stopped what they
26  were doing to stare at us. One of the boys called out, "Hey,
27  it's Beauty and the Beast!" Doreen ran out of the room cry-
28  ing. *(Pause)* She wasn't the only one...
29
30
31
32
33
34
35

# Living on the Edge

1     Just for one second, one nanosecond, one hundred mil-
2 lionth of a nanosecond, I wish I could be popular. It's got to be
3 so great. I imagine it's something like this: You get on the bus.
4 Everyone has saved you a seat so all you have to do is pick the
5 choicest spot. That person feels honored that you decided to sit
6 next to them and gives you the dessert out of their lunch bag.
7 You get to school and this big group of girls is waiting for you
8 to tell you the latest and juiciest gossip firsthand, like moments
9 after the fact, never months after. The cutest boy on your team
10 walks up to you with a single rose he's cut from his mother's
11 garden. He reads you this poem he wrote especially for you in
12 front of the bus crowd. Everybody is laughing and giggling,
13 not 'cause it's like queer or anything, but because it's so, like,
14 romantic and stuff. You take the rose and he escorts you to
15 your locker. He opens it for you and carries your books to your
16 first period class. The teacher smiles at you 'cause you make a
17 cute couple and you know that nothing so cool has even hap-
18 pened to that teacher before. Everyone saves you a seat at
19 lunch. At the end of the day, the cutest boy kisses you really
20 gently like Prince Charming in *Sleeping Beauty,* not like some
21 stupid middle school boy who's trying to ram his tongue down
22 your throat. You get back on the bus and each day after is like
23 something out of a movie.
24     No, really, there's this girl at our school and her life has got
25 to be like that. I even saw the rose and poem bit with my own
26 two eyes. They only thing was like she acted all mad and
27 embarrassed that Josh, the cutest boy, would ever make such
28 a scene. She might be pretty, but she's gotta be nuts not to like
29 that kind of attention.
30     Nothing so wonderful has ever happened to me. I'm not

1    like the bottom of the popularity barrel, but nobody is
2    opening my locker either. I'm OK-looking. I even had a
3    boyfriend once. His name was Derek and was a lot like me.
4    Just OK. I guess I liked him enough. His friend Brian came
5    up to me in homeroom and asked me if I'd go out with
6    Derek. Since I wasn't doing anything else, I said sure. We
7    went out for two whole weeks before I broke up with him.
8    He figured that one week's worth of dating was like the
9    equivalent of one base per week. Ya know, like first base,
10   second base, third base, and…? Kissing him was OK. His
11   breath was all right. But the next Monday he French kissed
12   me. Gross! Kissing was fine, but every kiss after Monday he
13   expected to ram his tongue down my throat. I hated knowing
14   what he had for lunch. By Friday he was already inching his
15   hand under my T-shirt. No way! So I broke up with him.
16   After that he told all the guys that I was straight, so there
17   went my whole middle school dating career in one shot.
18       I stand on the edge and imagine what it would be like to
19   be one of the popular kids. I know exactly what kinda per-
20   son I would be if I was popular. What I would do, what I
21   would say, who I would go out with. But popularity is kinda
22   like a maze. You get to be popular if you get to the center,
23   and I'm stuck in a dead end.
24
25
26
27
28
29
30
31
32
33
34
35

# Be Home at Dark
## and Other Ridiculous Rules

1    *(On phone)* OK, Mom. I said OK! Yes, we'll be careful.
2    We're always careful. Mommm. I never talk to strangers...at
3    least not the ugly ones. I'm kidding, I'm only kidding. Sheesh!
4    Can't you take a joke? OK. *(Pause)* OK! OK, nine thirty. See
5    you then. I love you too. *(Hangs up the phone.)*
6        Don't talk to strangers! Don't forget to call! Do you have
7    a quarter? Be home by dark! You'd think I lived in a prison!
8    I figure by the time I'm fifty I should finally be allowed to go
9    on a date without asking my parents' permission first. It seems
10   that the moment I turned thirteen, I suddenly became untrust-
11   worthy and irresponsible. I'm not a baby anymore. I can't see
12   why my parents can't give me a little more freedom.
13       My cousin, Holly, has it so easy. She's the youngest and has
14   all these older brothers and sisters. Whenever she wants to do
15   something she can always find someone to drive her to the
16   mall or take her to the skating rink. The crazy thing is that her
17   mom lets her! My aunt figures that if she's with someone older,
18   she'll be fine. No such luck for me. I'm the oldest in my family
19   and I never get to do anything. I'm not allowed to talk on the
20   phone after eight. I have to be in bed by nine-thirty on school
21   nights. I'm not allowed to wear eye makeup, only lip gloss. No
22   boy is ever allowed to come over if my parents aren't home and
23   God forbid, we can never, for one second, be alone together. My
24   mom even picks out all my clothes, including my bathing suits.
25   I swear I will never set foot on the beach in that navy blue
26   sailor suit thing my mom bought last year at McRoberts. I'll
27   have to hide it until I'm in college.
28       One rare, blissful evening my parents agreed to let me stay
29   out until eleven, but that was only because I was going to a
30   Christmas dance at school. Picture this storybook ending: The

1  clock strikes eleven and my prince kisses me goodnight to
2  the blaring sound of my dad's car horn. I could've died.
3      I know lots of kids at school who sneak out after their
4  parents have gone to bed. They walk around and hang out
5  at the 7-11 and it sounds like they have a great time. Believe
6  me, the thought has crossed my mind, but the only problem
7  is that I can't think of what I would do once I got out. And
8  if I got caught, I'd be in such big trouble. Jay, my boyfriend,
9  can't stay out past nine-thirty either, so why bother, and did I
10  mention that I would be in big trouble? OK, so maybe a curfew
11  isn't the end of the world, but next summer, I'm drawing a
12  line in the sand over any bathing suit with a skirt!
13
14
15
16
17
18
19
20
21
22
23
24
25
26
27
28
29
30
31
32
33
34
35

# Home Sweet Home

1    *(Running On-stage and chanting)* **There's no place like**
2    **home, there's no place like home. Auntie Em, Auntie Em.**
3    **There's no place like home.**
4    **What were we thinking? I ask you, would any sensible,**
5    **responsible, punctual, no, not punctual, eighth grade girl risk**
6    **life, limb and possibly the grounding of a lifetime over a stu-**
7    **pid high school boy? Members of the jury, be swift and**
8    **merciful in your judgment because if you don't, my parents**
9    **are surely going to kill me!**
10    **It's all Shannon's fault. It was her stupid idea. I normally**
11    **don't agree to stupid ideas, but this stupid idea included**
12    **Jonathan.** *(Big, dramatic sigh)* **Yeah, like I'll ever be able to see**
13    **him in this lifetime without the bars on my windows ruining**
14    **the view. What were we thinking? See, Shannon knows this**
15    **boy, Michael, whose best friend is Chad and Chad is**
16    **Jonathan's brother and Chad told Michael when he was talk-**
17    **ing with Michael and Shannon that he and Jonathan would**
18    **meet Michael at the 7-11 around midnight to pick him up. Got**
19    **that? Jonathan is proof that God is a woman because no man**
20    **could make a creature this perfect. He's beautiful. So after her**
21    **parents went to bed, Shannon snuck over to my house and**
22    **knocked on my window. Thank goodness my bedroom is on**
23    **the ground floor because sneaking out of a second-story win-**
24    **dow is out of the question. I don't do heights.**
25    **OK, so we're walking down the sidewalk in my neighbor-**
26    **hood toward the 7-11. We can see the red seven glowing in the**
27    **distance. We're talking and laughing, planning what we're**
28    **gonna say to Jonathan when this car starts following us. Real**
29    **slow and creepy-like. We started to walk faster, but the car**
30    **pulled up next to us. This weird guy rolls down his window**

1   and asks us if we know where Green Leaf Drive is. Well,
2   duh, it's the road that we're on but Shannon stops to tell
3   him. Can you believe it? She leans over to talk in the win-
4   dow and he grabs her arm. She starts screaming, I start
5   screaming. Shannon grabs me and I try to pull her away
6   but I slip on the grass. The weirdo opens the car door and
7   Shannon shakes him loose. We both start running and
8   screaming down the street toward the 7-11. So much for a
9   dignified entrance. Jonathan, Chad, and Michael come run-
10  ning up to meet us. We're crying and blubbering and
11  Shannon's arm is bleeding. Fortunately, some cop was also
12  there getting coffee. I've never been so happy to see a mem-
13  ber of the law enforcement services in my whole life. He
14  writes down all the info we can remember about the guy
15  and puts out a warrant for his arrest. He also gave us a lec-
16  ture about walking around at night. He must be a parent.
17  Then he took us home. I probably don't have to tell you
18  what happened when a police officer drops me off at home
19  in a police car at twelve-thirty on a school night when I'm
20  supposed to be in bed fast asleep. Let's just say I won't see
21  daylight again until I'm at least fifty. Still, there's no place
22  like home!
23
24
25
26
27
28
29
30
31
32
33
34
35

# Mary's Pregnant... I Think

1       There's this girl, Mary, in our school who really thinks
2  she's the stuff. I mean, she must think she's fifteen and the
3  queen of the universe. Mary has these gigantic boobs and
4  always wears these tight little shirts so all the boys can see
5  what she's got. She wears tons of makeup and has big, hair-
6  spray hair. When she walks, you'd think she was walking a
7  zig-zag her hips swing so much. I mean, total slut. Mary's
8  always hanging out with the guys and won't talk to us girls.
9  Not even if you are sharing a mirror with her in the bathroom.
10  All of us other girls swap brushes and combs and lipstick and
11  stuff. Mary's got this bag full of makeup — a whole cosmetic
12  counter and never once has she offered to share it with any of
13  us. Not that we would take it 'cause you never know what you
14  might catch from her.
15       Anyway, last week Mary starts wearing all these really
16  baggy tops and sweat pants. Come on, sweat pants in May? I
17  didn't know she even owned anything baggy. She's stopped
18  wearing tons of makeup and it looks like her hair hasn't seen
19  a brush in weeks. Marco, the guy Mary was hanging all over a
20  couple of weeks ago, moved to Chicago on Friday. The other
21  guys in their group are kinda ignoring her. Like, they're being
22  nice and all, but not drooling over her the way that they used
23  to. Mary's not acting like she's the stuff anymore 'cause
24  Mary's pregnant...I think.
25
26
27
28
29
30

# He Said He Loved Me...

1     I know what the girls call me and it really hurts. I've never
2    felt comfortable around girls and for good reasons. They act so
3    sweet to your face and then the minute you walk away, they
4    tear you down. I have six brothers at home, so naturally I feel
5    better hanging out with guys. But hanging around guys is
6    enough to give you a reputation even if nothing's going on.
7    When you've got breasts, forget it. They carve your name in
8    stone.
9    I never wanted this body. I never even wanted to be a girl.
10  I never wanted to do girl stuff or have girl-type things, but can
11  you imagine my mom's delight to finally get a daughter on the
12  seventh try? She's the one who's always dolling me up, telling
13  me to "play up my features." I want overalls; she buys mini-
14  skirts. I want T-shirts; she buys tank tops. "Wear it while
15  you're young and beautiful," Mama tells me. I feel like I have
16  to do what she says, so I smile and squeeze myself into the
17  clothes of the person she'd like me to be.
18  The other girls have always avoided me and that's just
19  fine. But I hate being talked about. When Marco said he loved
20  me, I thought, "Hey, this is OK." It was like hanging out with
21  my brothers but better. My brothers never made my skin tin-
22  gle. Marco made all the abuse from those snotty girls seem
23  worth it. When he said he'd take care of everything, I believed
24  him. That's what it means to be a guy, taking charge of things.
25  I was stupid to believe that all guys follow through. I've seen
26  my brothers make enough mistakes to know this isn't always
27  the case, but because Marco said he loved me, I thought he was
28  different. I always expected the girls to let me down, but now
29  one of the guys has, too. Marco didn't take care of everything
30  and now I have to take care of myself. My mom's not dressing

1   me like a girl any more. Now, for the first time, she's wish-
2   ing I were a boy. More than ever, so am I.
3
4
5
6
7
8
9
10
11
12
13
14
15
16
17
18
19
20
21
22
23
24
25
26
27
28
29
30
31
32
33
34
35

# And
# Gentlemen...

# P.U. or Why I Hate PE

1    PE stinks. No, really, I mean stinks. Can you imagine a
2  more foul-smelling place on the whole planet than the boys'
3  locker room in a middle school? Only a high school could pos-
4  sibly be more smelly. Not that the girls' room smells good,
5  mind you (I wouldn't know) but it's got to smell better than
6  the guys'! They've got all that stuff to spray on — hair spray,
7  perfume, deodorant even. So it's got to smell better.
8    I've always been a clean type of guy. Personal hygiene is
9  very important if you want to make it with the ladies. But I was
10  clean way before that, too. As far as I know, my family doesn't
11  have any pictures of me with Spaghetti-Os all over my face or
12  punching a birthday cake with my fist. *(Lowers voice and looks*
13  *around.)* My mom even told me that she potty-trained me in one
14  day because I hated to be messy. Gross. I learned to do my laun-
15  dry when I was eight 'cause my mom couldn't keep up with me,
16  and I iron all my clothes except my socks. You get the picture.
17    Now, here I am in middle school, forced to endure the odif-
18  erous horror known as Physical Education. I like to play
19  sports and I really don't mind the exercise thing. When I'm
20  home, I just go shower, but would you want to strip down in
21  front of a locker room full of fourteen-year-olds? My best
22  friend, Kevin Smith, did on the first day of school, and they're
23  still calling him a fag. Do they think it's manly to smell like a
24  wet dog? That girls are attracted to sweat instead of Old
25  Spice? Go figure. Andy Thompson is some kind of hero to
26  these guys because he hasn't washed his gym clothes since our
27  last report card. You can't get near his row of lockers without
28  gagging. And believe me, you don't want to be downwind of
29  him on the playing field. Come to think of it, that must be his
30  team's strategy.

1      I, on the other hand, would rather be squeaky clean
2  than squeak into home anyday.
3
4
5
6
7
8
9
10
11
12
13
14
15
16
17
18
19
20
21
22
23
24
25
26
27
28
29
30
31
32
33
34
35

# Jungle Gym Fever

1  Next to lunch, PE is the best part of going to school. Who-
2  ever said that kids had to play games and get a grade for it
3  should have a country named after them. Our coach, Coach
4  Biggins, or Mr. B, is the greatest. He's tough on us 'cause he
5  likes to see us win. Some parents think he's too strict and too
6  set on winning, but hey, who doesn't like to win?
7  My favorite sport in PE is kickball. Lots of guys would say
8  football, but it's only flag football and that's for wimps. Kick-
9  ball has more strategy than you think. Sometimes you aim for a
10  player then kick the ball so hard that it knocks the wind out of
11  him, or better yet, bounces off and heads for no-man's land.
12  That's great. My favorite trick, though, is to act like I'm going
13  to really send the ball flying and then only give it a baby tap.
14  The pitcher has to run like mad for it and by the time he catch-
15  es up with it, I'm safely on first or second base at least. Lately,
16  the games have been close, too close, so I came up with a secret
17  strategy: I haven't washed my gym clothes in nine weeks. Boy,
18  are they ripe. They almost make me sick when I put them on,
19  but slowly I get used to it. When I play first base, the runner
20  usually can't wait to get away from me, so he leads off early.
21  Man, I can't tell you how many guys we've gotten out that way.
22  Basketball is cool. Volleyball is OK if we can spike the ball.
23  I love to run the mile. I like to push myself and feel my heart
24  pumping really hard. Just when I think my legs are going to
25  turn to Jell-O, and I can't breathe anymore, all of a sudden I
26  feel as if I could run forever. You need to learn to push yourself,
27  though. It doesn't just happen. Mr. B tells me that only the best
28  athletes can use their minds to force their bodies to go past the
29  point of resistance. I plan on being one of those athletes. I want
30  to be the best at something else besides lunch.

# Sports Jock and Couch Potato

1     *(Both boys enter from opposite sides of the stage and cross at*
2  *center as if meeting in a hallway. SPORTS JOCK is in a hurry;*
3  *COUCH POTATO is simply meandering. While one monolog is*
4  *being spoken, the other player remains motionless.)*
5  **SPORTS: Ronnie, I've been looking all over for you.**
6     **Where've you been? Soccer tryouts are in twenty min-**
7     **utes and you haven't even signed up yet.**
8  **COUCH: Aw, I've decided not to go out for soccer. I got other**
9     **stuff to do.**
10  **SPORTS: Like what? Finishing off a can of Pringles while**
11     **you watch** *Wheel of Fortune***?**
12  **COUCH: You're funny, man. Besides, I got lots to do that**
13     **doesn't involve getting sweaty. I'll catch you later.**
14  **SPORTS: Come on, you never want to do stuff with me any-**
15     **more...**
16  **COUCH: Whatever. See ya.**
17     *(Both boys cross to separate sides of the playing area.*
18     *SPORTS JOCK presents his monolog first.)*
19  **SPORTS: I just don't get him. A couple of years ago, we**
20  **did everything together. We even met at basketball camp. He**
21  **was a guard and I was the center for Dunlop's Demons. Now I**
22  **bet he couldn't tell ya how many guys are supposed to be on**
23  **the court at one time!**
24    **To me, sports is a way of life. I get such a rush out of com-**
25  **peting in the game, any game. What is it? The thrill of victory**
26  **and the agony of defeat? That's what I like about sports. It's**
27  **an all or nothing existence. You're either a winner or a loser.**
28    **I play sports all year round. In the spring, it's time to start**
29  **training for baseball. Then it's soccer and football season. By**
30  **the time it gets too cold to be outside, I'm indoors playing**

1    basketball. I can't seem to get enough. After one sport ends
2    and there's this lull before the next one starts, I drive my
3    mom crazy slam-dunking the laundry or hitting paper
4    towel wads into the trash can with a broom.
5        I really like team sports, but I'm just as happy compet-
6    ing with myself. I love to swim and ride my bike. For
7    Christmas, I got a pair of in-line skates. Bowling is cool and
8    I love to play golf. It's basically baseball on the ground. Just
9    as long as I can dribble, hit, pitch, swing, or stroke, I'm
10   happy.
11       I have to admit, one of the reasons I think I like sports
12   is because I'm good at them. I'm what you call a "natural."
13   But even "naturals" have to practice. That's the thing that
14   bugs me about Ronnie. Whenever we used to play together,
15   he'd get mad at me if I was better at a game than he was.
16   Remember how we met at basketball camp? We had a free-
17   throw contest and I won! He got all mad and wouldn't talk
18   to me for two days 'cause he said I showed him up. Not like
19   it was hard. My blind grandmother could shoot better with
20   one hand tied behind her back. He never practiced. I shot
21   fifty free-throws every day for a week before the contest. It
22   doesn't take a rocket scientist to figure out who stood a bet-
23   ter chance of winning.
24       Lately, Ronnie's been blowing me off whenever I ask
25   him to join up. "I've got stuff to do…" Yeah, like demolish-
26   ing fourteen boxes of cookies during the reruns of
27   *Baywatch*. Boy, is he getting fat. He used to be so involved.
28       Not me. You won't catch me slacking off. I'd rather be
29   part of life than just watch it go by on a TV screen. The only
30   thing is I'd like to play a little one-on-one every now and
31   then rather than practice jumpshots by myself. It's a little
32   hard to rebound the ball to yourself…
33       *(SPORTS JOCK freezes and COUCH POTATO speaks his*
34   *mind.)*
35       **COUCH:** What is with that guy? He thinks he's Mr.

1   Super Sport or something. Baseball, soccer, wrestling, track
2   meets. Anything to get all sweaty and breathe hard. Per-
3   sonally, I can think of much better ways to spend my time.
4   Just because I used to play all those dumb games doesn't
5   mean that I necessarily want to do it now. A person can
6   change, you know.
7       I was never really good at sports. OK, so I never wanted
8   to be, but I'm not like what you'd call athletically inclined.
9   My parents made me 'cause my dad used to be this sports
10  jock in college. Got like all kinds of MVP awards and stuff.
11  You know the saying, "Like father, like son"? A stranger on
12  the street has a better chance of acting more like my dad.
13  I'm a lousy athlete. I could practice fielding for hours and
14  hours and still never catch one pop-up. "Just keep your eye
15  on the ball, Son." If I had four eyes straight across my fore-
16  head, it wouldn't help. I'd only end up getting hit in the
17  head which I can say from experience is enough to make
18  you want to smother the inventor of the game in peanuts
19  and cracker jacks.
20      Fortunately, my sister was born and she shows some
21  promise of Dad's gift. Now she's the lucky one they drag off
22  to swim meets and gymnastic competitions. This is just fine
23  with me since it leaves me with plenty of time to enjoy my
24  real love — TV.
25      I don't just like TV, I live and breathe it. If Hunter
26  cheats on Marigold during an episode of *California Nights*,
27  I feel her pain. I love to root for the defending champion on
28  *Jeopardy* and laugh with the goof-balls on *Saturday Night*
29  *Live*. Lots of people consider watching TV a waste of time.
30  If that's so, I can probably guarantee that there are more
31  injured athletes who are wasting their recovery time with
32  the boob tube than there are couch potatoes shushing down
33  snowy mountain slopes.
34      Greg is good at sports and that's great for him. I'd be
35  happy to cheer for him in the stands…if he'd just give me a

1    little bit of credit for knowing the answer to the $20,000
2    question.
3    *(SPORTS JOCK unfreezes and rejoins the scene.)*
4    SPORTS:  Hey, Ronnie. Ya know they canceled football
5        practice 'cause the coach had to go out of town. What
6        are ya doing this weekend?
7    COUCH:  My parents have to take my sister to Regionals.
8        I'm gonna stay home. The *Star Wars* trilogy is on cable.
9    SPORTS:  I've never seen all three. Are they any good?
10    COUCH:  Are they any good? My young Jedi, you have
11        much to learn. Listen, I'll make a deal with you. If you
12        come over and watch this science fiction masterpiece
13        with me, I'll see if I can't remember how to whip your
14        butt in a little one-on-one during the breaks.
15    SPORTS:  You're on! *(Pause)* Did you say whip my butt? I
16        seem to remember…
17    *(Boys walk off together playfully ribbing each other.)*
18
19
20
21
22
23
24
25
26
27
28
29
30
31
32
33
34
35

# Moneybags

1     My old man is loaded! Hey, it's no secret. He bleeds hun-
2  dred dollar bills when he cuts himself shaving. I'm not really
3  sure what his job is, but he's gone all the time. I think it has
4  something to do with buying stuff. Not like stocks, but like
5  buildings or something, maybe companies. Can somebody buy
6  companies? Anyway, he makes a killing.
7     We live in this really big house up in High Grove Estates.
8  It has a game room with a pool table and a home theater sys-
9  tem. We've got a pool that has a slide built into the
10  landscaping. It looks like a waterfall coming down the rocks,
11  but if you get out and go around back, you'll see stairs up to
12  the top of the waterfall. My mom designed it. She said any
13  other kind of slide would look tacky. I've got my own room
14  and bathroom. If I wanted, I would never have to leave my
15  room. I've got a phone, a TV, a VCR, a computer, and my own
16  video game unit. But I have to go down to eat. That's a rule.
17  One time I left a glass of milk on the floor and the maid kicked
18  it over when she came up to clean my room. Now normally this
19  wouldn't be a big deal, but the milk was old and kinda thick
20  and chunky and the maid slipped on that glop and broke a hip.
21  My dad said that's just the sort of opportunity those kind of
22  people look for 'cause we could get sued. Dad's always worried
23  about that, getting sued. So now I can't eat in my room.
24     My friends always want to come over to my house. I have
25  extra bikes and stuff. We have our own trampoline. My friends
26  like it 'cause they can have their own room which connects to
27  mine through the bathroom. Most of my friends have to share
28  a room at home. My mom lets us stay up late and she'll take us
29  to the grocery store and we can pick out whatever we want to
30  eat. Not like dinner stuff 'cause we have someone to do that,

1    but candy and chips and stuff. My friend David comes over
2    the most. He says it's like a holiday. He's got five brothers
3    and sisters and they live in this really small house. I've only
4    been over there once. It was dirty and crowded and the
5    baby was always crying. I told David's mom that she should
6    get a maid like my mom and then her house wouldn't be so
7    dirty. She turned all red and said that my mom was very
8    lucky to have married a man who made so much money
9    that she could afford a maid. David told me I hurt his
10   mom's feelings. That she cleaned all the time, but with so
11   many kids it just got messed up easily. I felt bad. I told
12   David's mom that she could borrow our maid for the day to
13   give herself a break. She just got all red again and walked
14   away. I haven't been back there since. That's OK with me.
15   I don't like graham crackers and juice for a snack anyway.
16   Besides, they don't even have a big screen TV. That family
17   needs to get their priorities straight. *(Walks Off-stage shaking*
18   *his head.)*
19
20
21
22
23
24
25
26
27
28
29
30
31
32
33
34
35

# The Blue Light Special

1     *(Voice Off-stage)* **Attention, Kmart shoppers — our blue**
2    **light special on a twelve-pack of Jiffy toilet paper is now on**
3    **sale in aisle three. Be sure to have your purchase tagged before**
4    **leaving the area.**
5     My mom shops here all the time and she lives to hear those
6    announcements. I'm living proof. Here I stand in my "blue
7    light" sneakers over "blue light" socks and "blue light" under-
8    wear. Do you know how embarrassing it is to have a mom that
9    gets excited over a special on underwear? I dread the fact that
10   I may see one of the kids from school, but that isn't very likely.
11   Most of the kids that go there are rich. I mean, really rich.
12   Oozing richness. That kind doesn't usually shop at Kmart.
13   *(Pause)* Unless of course it was the last store on the planet and
14   they had to max out their credit cards before they died.
15   *(Laughs at own joke.)*
16    My family is not in that group. I have five brothers and sis-
17   ters. My dad drives a truck and makes pretty good money, but
18   six kids eat a lot. My mom stays home to take care of all of us
19   and make sure that we don't get into trouble. She says it's
20   more important to her and Dad that we grow up to be good
21   people instead of having a lot of extra things and being jerks.
22    We have a nice house. It's small, but we aren't like sleep-
23   ing ten to a room. I share a room with my little brother,
24   George. He's pretty cool for four. He keeps his Legos on his
25   side of the room and that's a pretty big responsibility for some-
26   one that little. My mom refinished a lot of our furniture from
27   Goodwill and yard sales. My favorite chair in the living room
28   even came from the trash. Someone was just gonna throw it out
29   but my mom stopped and asked if she could have it. They even
30   helped her load it in the car. I guess she's really resourceful,

1   but I wish she'd stay out of other people's trash. The worst
2   part was when my friend Alex came over. He said his mom
3   used to have a chair that looked just like it. I didn't say any-
4   thing, but I could've died.
5        Alex has an excellent house. He has his own room and
6   bathroom. He's got a phone and TV and lots of other cool
7   stuff too. I love going over there 'cause it's like a vacation. I
8   really love my family, but sometimes it's nice to get away.
9   Alex came over to my house once. I figured since he's an
10  only child it would be neat for him to have so many people
11  around. He didn't think so. He kept asking me how could I
12  stand living with so many people in such a small space. He
13  even told my mom she should get a maid so her house
14  wouldn't be so dirty. That made me mad. Mom really tries
15  to keep it clean but with eight people, it's practically impos-
16  sible. After that, I figured it would be easier if I just went
17  over to Alex's house. *(Pause)* Ya know, his house is cool and
18  all, but I still like coming home the best. Being a "blue light
19  special" kid is hard, but since my family puts all the empha-
20  sis on "special," it's worth it.
21
22
23
24
25
26
27
28
29
30
31
32
33
34
35

# Fat Kid

Just say it — I'm fat. I'm not plump or chubby or stout like my Grandmother calls me. I'm fat. You know it, I know it, let's just deal with it, all right?

I've always been fat. I was a fat baby. My fat even had fat. I've seen pictures. I looked more like the Michelin tire man than a baby. Just rolls and rolls of fat all piled up together. My eyes looked squinty 'cause my cheeks were so fat. But everyone seems to think that a fat baby is cute. No one stares or points or calls a fat baby bad names. Everyone wants to hold you and squeeze you 'cause to them, you're just a big, squishy pillow in baby blue clothes. I even got to be in a magazine ad 'cause I was so doughy and cute. "Keep baby's skin newborn soft with Miller's Baby Lotion — Large or small, Miller's fits all." They put me next to this skinny, little kid. It's one of those naked-baby-on-a-blanket ads. It's weird how scrawny that skinny baby looks. I look so much healthier and stuff. Like you would want to hold me if you had a choice. That toothpick baby looks like he would break if you hugged him too hard.

Once you get to elementary school, forget it. No one wants to hug you or put you in a magazine. Everyone starts calling you "Fat Kid." "Hey, the Fat Kid is crying" or "Pass the Fat Kid the red paint," or the worst, "Don't pick the Fat Kid. We want Danny on our team instead." It's like if you have this layer of fat, you're no good. That you don't have feelings that could get hurt.

By the times I got to the sixth grade, fat was like part of my name. Like Mister, only Fatty. Now that I'm in eighth, I don't give a crap what they call me. No matter how many times I've told them my name, they still call me Fatty. They'll always call me Fatty. I'll never be a person to them, so I stay out of their

1    way and they stay out of mine. I even had the doctor write
2    me a note excusing me from PE. Heart problems, it said. So
3    now I don't have to be a burden on anyone's team. I'm an
4    office aid instead. I take notes around to teachers and file
5    things for the secretaries. It's easy. Plus, on my report card,
6    I don't have to deal with the PE teacher's comment:
7    "Weight interferes with mobility." I get, "Polite and helpful
8    young man." It's a nice change.
9        Actually, I could deal with the things the guys say if I
10   had to. It's the girls. There's this one girl, Ashley. She is so
11   fine. She's a cheerleader and she has this really nice long,
12   blond hair. I sit behind her in Social Studies. It's an
13   assigned seat. If it wasn't assigned, I really don't think Ashley
14   would sit there. She's friendly to my face and all; she's too
15   nice and cool not to be, but no one usually wants to sit next
16   to me — most of all a fine girl like her. Once I passed a
17   group of girls in the hall while delivering a pass to another
18   teacher and she was with them. I said, "Hi, Ashley." She
19   didn't say anything to me, but she smiled. When the group
20   of them thought I couldn't hear them anymore, one of them
21   said, "He's so gross. His butt probably doesn't fit in the
22   desks." And Ashley told her, "Yeah, I'd rather die than be
23   seen with a fat guy."
24        Hey, girls, just because I'm fat doesn't mean I can't
25   hear. *(Pause)* It also doesn't mean that I don't have a heart.
26
27
28
29
30
31
32
33
34
35

# Stringbean

1     *(Voices Off-stage)*
2         "Stretch!"
3         "Hey, Stringbean!"
4         "How's the weather up there, big guy?"
5     *(Walks On-stage calling back smart remark.)* **Your mama**
6 **said the temperature is fine and she'll send ya a postcard when**
7 **I decide to give her a break.**
8     **I'm the tallest kid in High Grove Middle School. No, really.**
9 **The coaches measured us last spring in PE. Most of the kids on**
10 **the locker room wall were all about the same size** *(Indicates flat*
11 *line with hand)* **and then there's me.** *(Hand shoots up.)* **I'm thir-**
12 **teen, six feet, three inches, and my doctor says I'm not done**
13 **growing yet.**
14     **As you can guess, I get a lot of basketball comments. Peo-**
15 **ple think that if you're tall that you automatically like the**
16 **game. I always get picked first to play center. The truth is, I**
17 **hate the game. I'd rather play with my computer or build**
18 **rocket models. Nobody asks you how tall you are on the inter-**
19 **net, or gives you these whistles like you're a freak or**
20 **something. On the internet, everybody is the same size.**
21     **My parents never expected me to grow like this. Everyone**
22 **in my family is normal size. My sister's even closer to midget**
23 **status than most kids but people don't look at her and stare.**
24 **It's just some runaway mutant gene. And it's not like I'm tall**
25 **and muscular either. I'm a wimp. Starving greyhounds look**
26 **fatter than I do. I drink these nutrition power shakes. I lift**
27 **weights. But I'm still skinny. And it makes me look taller, too,**
28 **which is just what I need. But even though most toddlers could**
29 **beat me up, no one messes with me. I guess if you're tall, you**
30 **look more like a grown-up. Either that or if you don't have a**

1    head where everyone can see you, you don't count. Not with
2    the guys. Not with the girls. Only the teachers look at you
3    and they talk to you like you're an adult. It's so unfair.
4       Last summer, our family took a trip out to California.
5    The best part of the trip was when we went to the Redwood
6    National Forest. They have trees there that have been grow-
7    ing for thousands of years. They are as tall as the sky 'cause
8    they're all competing for the sun. The shorter ones get shad-
9    ed out and die. One tree was so big we drove our car
10    through it. It was really cool to feel so small. I felt like the
11    passenger on one of my model rockets. For a second, I was
12    just like everybody else. The trees looked so tall and proud,
13    reaching higher and higher toward the clouds. They didn't
14    slouch to try to fit in a desk built for someone half their
15    height. They just grew and grew. Now, when I'm back in
16    school, and all the kids and teachers are down below my
17    shoulders, I close my eyes and try to pretend that I am a
18    Redwood. I am closer to the sun.
19
20
21
22
23
24
25
26
27
28
29
30
31
32
33
34
35

# Badge of Honor

1   If an office referral is like a badge of honor, then I'm as
2   decorated as a Christmas tree! I don't try to get in trouble.
3   Somehow, trouble just finds me. Like yesterday, yesterday was
4   bad from the time I got up to the time I went to bed.
5       When I got up, I forgot that I had to bring in some colored
6   pencils for math 'cause we're doing graphing. My mom ran
7   around yelling at me that I shouldn't wait until the last minute
8   to tell her these things and that I should be more responsible.
9   I hear this lecture all the time. We finally found some crayons
10  in my brother's toy box. Mom said they would have to do. I
11  decided I wasn't gonna use some baby crayons when every-
12  body else was using colored pencils, so I left them on the bus.
13  When I got to Math, Mr. Simmons yelled at me for not being
14  prepared and gave me an "alternate assignment." Think busy
15  work. And I still got a zero for the graphing assignment! At
16  lunch Ashley broke up with me 'cause she said she liked Tony
17  better now. Then Tony walked up and said, "Don't break his
18  heart. He might cry," and he does this big scene like he's pre-
19  tending to cry. When I started to walk away, he said, "Look at
20  the baby run away!" Well, nobody calls me a baby, so I walked
21  up to him and asked him why he was messing with me. He says
22  he didn't mess with babies, that babies were the ones that
23  messed their pants, and babies didn't mess up Tony. He's act-
24  ing all big and bad in front of Ashley, so I had to hit him. That
25  shut him up real fast. Then he jumped me and pretty soon I'm
26  in the office for starting a fight. I'm the one getting suspended
27  for three days 'cause of that punk.
28      When school got out, I had to stay after to collect all the
29  work I was gonna miss 'cause I'm suspended. Tony's friends
30  were waiting for me when I came out of my building. They

1  kinda followed me toward the bus loop making these crying
2  noises the whole time. When we got to the bus loop, they
3  pulled the fire alarm and ran off. The custodians and some
4  of the other teachers came running. Now I'm getting
5  blamed for that, too. It's just not fair. Stuff like that hap-
6  pens to me all the time. The vice-principal said that there
7  were witnesses that I was the one who pulled the alarm and
8  he named Tony's buddies. They said that they were coming
9  back to campus 'cause one of them forgot a book or some-
10 thing and they saw me do it. Their story is such crap.
11 What's an even bigger load is that all these adults believe
12 them. They say that they're honest young men and that I
13 had a motive to do it. What is this, like a crime story or
14 something? A motive? Get real! The worst part about it is
15 that the school is pressing charges 'cause it's a felony to
16 mess with those things and so I'm up for expulsion too.
17 When I got home, my mom said she'd had it with me and
18 was looking into sending me to military school. I thought
19 she was joking, but she, like, had all these pamphlets from
20 different schools and all. "No son of mine is going to embar-
21 rass this family. You'll learn respect if it kills you!" Actually,
22 death may be better. At least I'd stay out of trouble that
23 way...
24
25
26
27
28
29
30
31
32
33
34
35

# 'Fraidycat

1   I'll admit it. I'm a wimp. Yup, you heard me. Wimp, wuss,
2   pansy, mama's boy, you name it. That's me and I'm proud of
3   it. Now I know a lot of guys would be embarrassed to admit
4   such a thing, but not me. Wanna know why? *(Conspiratorial*
5   *whisper)* Chicks dig wimps. No, really, trust me. It's true. Oh
6   sure, lots of guys try to act tough in front of the ladies, but not
7   me. Being wimpy gets you just as far in the long run. Maybe
8   further...
9       See, in the fifth grade I tried to be all big and bad and it
10  just got me beat up. I was in the office all the time and boy, was
11  my mom mad. She practically grounded me through high
12  school. This year I decided to play it safe. New school, new rep-
13  utation, last chance, according to Mom. Shape up or ship out,
14  that's what she said. So I did.
15      Middle school is a lot different than elementary school.
16  For starters, I'm way shorter than most of the guys. This
17  works in my favor for the wimp method. Tommy Adkins, this
18  big, old seventh grader who's about three light years taller
19  than me, shoved my head into the water fountain on the first
20  day of school. That first day changed my life. It made me the
21  wimp I am today.
22      Tommy started laughing at me and said, "Look at the lit-
23  tle sixth grade baby!" All these other guys began to gather
24  around like I was gonna start something with that moron.
25  Tommy said, "Watcha gonna do, baby? Stand there and cry?"
26  But then the most amazing thing happened, the thing that
27  made me the believer in wimpiness that I am today. This group
28  of eighth grade girls was walking by. The tallest and best-look-
29  ing one said, "Tommy, you are the biggest jerk. I can't believe
30  you have to pick on little sixth graders. I should get Randy to

1    come kick your ..." and then she used a word I can't repeat.
2    I found out later that Randy is like the toughest guy in
3    eighth grade not mention her boyfriend. Then she walked
4    up to me and said the most beautiful words I'll ever hear.
5    "Come on. I'll show you where your house office is so you
6    can report this creep. You can put me down as a witness. My
7    name is Courtney O'Brien." All her friends asked if I was
8    OK and said that I was cute and didn't I have gorgeous
9    eyes. What's your name? Do you have an older brother? I
10    was in heaven. A flock of beautiful women came to my res-
11    cue on the first day of middle school. I saw the headlines in
12    the school paper: Defenseless Boy Saved by Gorgeous Ama-
13    zons. Sign me up for wimpdom, I thought.
14        Then the second most amazing thing happened. The
15    sixth grade principal called Tommy into his office and put
16    him in isolation for the rest of the day. He said I was a very
17    mature young man for not stooping to Tommy's level and
18    fighting. A mature young man? Me? This was the best day
19    in the history of school! To top it all off, Courtney saw me
20    at the bus loop and introduced me to Randy. He said if any-
21    body messed with me to let him know. He'd take care of the
22    problem personally. He said it real cool-like, too. Courtney
23    winked at me and said she'd see me tomorrow. By the next
24    day, I'd achieved legendary status as a sixth grade wimp.
25    You gotta problem with that?
26
27
28
29
30
31
32
33
34
35

# Call Me Casanova

1     I'm a babe magnet, a junior Don Juan. I am "The Man."
2    You can call me Casanova. Mindy Matthews, the finest girl of
3    all at High Grove Middle School, said she'd go out with me.
4    Me, Dan Johnson, your everyday Joe, has just been elevated to
5    legend status. See, Mindy doesn't go out with just anybody.
6    Heck, she doesn't even hang out with just anybody. She's really
7    picky about the company she keeps, so if you're hanging with
8    Mindy Matthews, you're really somebody. That's me, Mr.
9    Somebody. Yesterday I was nothing but the PE field dirt on
10   the bottoms of her very expensive, incredibly beautiful feet.
11   Today though, I'm Dan Johnson, Boy Hero, Man of the Gods.
12      I've had a crush on her since like the second grade. I mean
13   like who hasn't, right? But last week, in a stroke of good for-
14   tune, Mrs. Martin paired us up in Social Studies to do a special
15   report on Egypt. Just the two of us. We have the highest aver-
16   ages in the class so we got this special assignment to challenge
17   us or something. All I know is that for the last five days when
18   everyone else has been listening to Mrs. Martin yak on and on
19   about major exports and bordering countries, I've been able
20   to sit in the Media Center all alone with Mindy.
21      You should see my table at lunch. It's packed with all these
22   guys who want to know every intimate detail of her life. She
23   doesn't talk a whole lot about herself, but I do know that she
24   bites her pencils all the way down to the point. See, she bor-
25   rowed one from me on Thursday and apologized for the teeth
26   marks when she returned it. Some kid offered me ten bucks
27   for it at lunch, but I'm not selling Mindy out. Besides, her gor-
28   geous lips touched it. She dots all her i's with little hearts, she
29   uses Finesse shampoo — I know 'cause my sister uses it too —
30   and Country Apple hand lotion — she put some on. She writes

59

1    in big loopy letters and is a really hard worker. She did all
2    the writing for our project even though I offered to do it. I
3    figured she wouldn't want a callus, but she said she likes to
4    write. Oh, and get this: she wants to be either a scientist or
5    an author when she grows up. Heck, she'll be famous!
6    Every guy in our class will buy her books.
7         Anyway, today as we were packing our stuff to go back
8    to class, I casually mentioned that we could put our infor-
9    mation on my computer and that way we could make it look
10   like a newspaper from ancient Egypt and that it wouldn't
11   be so boring like a report, and hey, maybe her mom could
12   bring her over on Saturday. She said, "Sure, that's a cool
13   idea." I think I might have passed out. I even kinda thought
14   that maybe our conversation didn't really happen, but
15   when we were getting on the bus, she said, "You forgot to
16   give me your phone number so I can call you about coming
17   over." All the guys on the bus just sort of stared at me with
18   their mouths hanging open. I can't remember how I got
19   home or what I did after. All I know is that in twenty-four
20   hours Mindy Matthews is going to be here in my house,
21   using my computer, drinking from my glasses and hanging
22   out with me. I could die tonight a happy man. "The Man,"
23   that is.
24
25
26
27
28
29
30
31
32
33
34
35

# Mindy, McDonald's and Me

1    Let's just say I'm no longer "The Man." My date with
2    Mindy was a disaster. A complete and utter failure. I don't
3    even want to think about going to school on Monday and hav-
4    ing to face her. Yesterday I was Dan Johnson, Boy Hero, Man
5    of the Gods. Today I'm Dan Johnson, Big Dumb Jerk With
6    Ketchup and Special Sauce on His T-shirt. My dating history
7    with Mindy is, well, history! I'm ruined. *(Puts head in hands or*
8    *bangs head on table or wall for dramatic effect.)* **Ouch!** *(Stops*
9    *banging and rubs head.)*
10   Saturday started out perfectly. My dad took my sisters on a
11   Girl Scout camping trip so it was just Mom and me. Mom's pret-
12   ty cool about staying out of the way when I've got company, so I
13   knew I'd have plenty of time to be alone with Mindy. Her mom
14   was bringing her over around four-thirty after some modeling
15   interview and would pick her up again at eight-thirty. I would
16   have four whole glorious hours alone with beautiful, intelli-
17   gent, gorgeous, serious Mindy.
18   I picked up my room so Mindy wouldn't think I was a
19   slob. I don't know if all girls care but I figured Mindy would.
20   Then I messed it up a little. I didn't want her to think I was
21   some neat freak or something. When everything was perfect, I
22   went to take a shower. My dad's razor was lying next to the
23   sink. I thought it would be a good idea to shave. Now keep in
24   mind that I don't usually shave for the ladies. *(Pause)* OK, so
25   I'd never shaved before in my whole life, but how hard could
26   it be? Besides, I wanted to impress Mindy. I thought she'd be
27   into mature guys. Everything went OK until I started the actual
28   shaving part. *(Demonstrates shaving and pantomimes cutting*
29   *chin with the razor.)* **My dad makes it look so easy!** Now my
30   chin is spouting blood like Old Faithful and my cheeks are all

1   red 'cause I think I pushed too hard. I felt like I had rug
2   burn on my face, so I decided to put on some astringent to
3   take away the sting. Big mistake. Now my chin is spouting
4   blood, my cheeks are fire engine red, and my eyes are
5   watering. This is when the doorbell rings. It's Mindy. She
6   looks gorgeous. I look like raw meat. Speaking of meat,
7   we'll skip to the source of my ultimate humiliation. Let's
8   just say that everything goes OK until we decide to go to
9   McDonald's.
10      Mom had slipped me ten bucks to take Mindy to
11  McDonald's for dinner. It's only a couple of blocks from my
12  house, so we walked. When we got there, I ordered a Big
13  Mac, large fries and a Coke. Mindy ordered a Happy Meal.
14  Isn't that cute? I carried our trays over to a nice private
15  table for two and we sat down to eat. And we sat and stared
16  and sat some more. I mean, up until now we'd talked about
17  school things: ancient Egypt, Mrs. Martin, my computer.
18  Boring stuff. But what do you say to the most beautiful girl
19  in the whole middle school over dinner? My mind was
20  blank but I didn't want her to think I was ignoring her, so I
21  smiled. Rule #1: Never smile while eating a Big Mac.
22      "You've got a big piece of lettuce stuck in your braces,"
23  she told me. Great. I got up and went to the bathroom to get
24  rid of the offending lettuce. When I came back, some high
25  school guy was in my seat. I casually strolled back to the
26  table and stepped on a package of ketchup. The ketchup
27  squirts Mindy, me, and the high school guy. I slip on the
28  ketchup and hit my head on the tile floor knocking myself
29  out. *(Bows to the audience.)* When I came to, Mindy was
30  standing over me like a guardian angel and some motherly
31  customer was patting my cheeks with a damp napkin. Very
32  dignified, indeed. To make matters worse, the high school
33  guy who turned out to be a friend of Mindy's sister offered
34  to give us a ride home. Who would you choose: mature high
35  school guy with a car or middle school kid with a dented

1     head? Mom freaked out when she saw the ketchup which
2     she thought was blood, called Mrs. Matthews to come get
3     Mindy right away and I spent the rest of the evening in
4     High Grove Medical's Emergency Room. All I have to show
5     for my date with Mindy is a newspaper from ancient Egypt,
6     and some stitches and ketchup stains, so please don't call
7     me Casanova. *(Puts head back in hands or back on table.)*
8
9
10
11
12
13
14
15
16
17
18
19
20
21
22
23
24
25
26
27
28
29
30
31
32
33
34
35

# June, July and August

1      The best thing about school is summer vacation. Whoever
2  would suggest that kids should go to school all year long has
3  either been out of school so long that they have forgotten how
4  horrible it is, or they are just plain mean.
5      Summer vacation is the only reward kids get for putting
6  up with boring, beat-up textbooks, daily rations of food poi-
7  soning in the cafeteria and hundred-year-old English teachers
8  who still think that correct spelling and punctuation is the only
9  way to get to heaven. When the bell rings on the last day of
10  school, it's as if the governor has called up and decided to let
11  you live, the guillotine gets stuck at the top, the loaded gun is
12  firing blanks. You get the picture. The doors open and you're
13  free to be the biggest, laziest slob on the face of the Earth. You
14  finally get to throw out all those bad test papers, the parent
15  conference note you conveniently forgot to give your mom,
16  and the love notes from girls you now hate. All of it. You don't
17  even have to carry that overgrown turtle shell you call a back-
18  pack until September. You are free, free, free. Free at last, free
19  at last. Thank God, the school year's past.
20      The only bad thing about summer vacation is waiting for
21  your final report card to arrive in the mail. The positive or
22  negative impact of this stupid government document could
23  make or break your summer vacation plans. Like when I was
24  in the fourth grade, I did bad. Really bad. When my parents
25  got the news, they got all worried that I would be held back so
26  they signed me up for summer school and hired me a tutor.
27  After I was done with all that, they sent me to computer camp.
28  It was without doubt the worst summer in my whole existence.
29      On the other hand, this summer I'm planning on having
30  the best summer in my whole life. As soon as the bell rings, my

1    family and I are leaving for California. We're driving cross-
2    country in a camper van. We're gonna camp, go hiking and
3    fishing. We're going to the Grand Canyon and go white-
4    water rafting. It will be so cool. We'll be gone for a whole
5    month. Then when we get back, my grandparents are com-
6    ing down to visit. They've promised to take me to
7    Adventure World which is just about the greatest theme
8    park on the planet. After they leave, my buddies and I have
9    plans to build a fort in the woods behind my house. If we do
10   a good job, our parents have already said we could sleep out
11   in it if we're careful.
12       Uh-oh. The final countdown. 10 — 9 — 8 — 7 — 6 — 5
13   — 4 — 3, 2, 1...Yahoo! No more pencils, no more books. No
14   more teachers' dirty looks! Summer, ready or not, here I
15   come! *(Runs Off-stage.)*
16
17
18
19
20
21
22
23
24
25
26
27
28
29
30
31
32
33
34
35

# The Smell of Chalk Dust, the Roar of the Crowd

1      I love school. You must be thinking, "What a dork!" But
2  really, think about it, school is great. I suppose summer vaca-
3  tion is cool and all, but toward the end of August, boredom sets
4  in big time. I usually just sit in front of the TV flipping through
5  the channels until the clock says I should go to sleep again. By
6  the time plaid and pencils start appearing in the stores, I'm
7  ready for a change.

8      The first day of school is the best. You put on a brand new
9  outfit carefully chosen for the big event — jeans so stiff it's
10  hard to bend at the waist, sneakers that squeak when you walk
11  down to the kitchen for breakfast. When the bus pulls up at
12  your stop, it's all shiny and new-looking. Somebody's washed,
13  waxed and painted it. Even the barf smell from the last day
14  is gone.

15      The bus isn't the only thing that smells new. It's hard to beat
16  the smell of a school on the first day back from summer vaca-
17  tion. The smell of the wax on the linoleum. The way a new
18  textbook smells before it's had a chance to fester in your locker
19  next to last week's PE clothes. I love the way a brand new #2
20  pencil smells as you sharpen it for the first time. It smells like
21  a new chance.

22      The teachers smile and act reasonably excited about their
23  subjects. Unless you've had a perfect brother or sister in the
24  grade before you, everyone starts with a clean slate. The teach-
25  ers look at you with possibility instead of shaking their heads
26  as you walk into the room. You look around for new faces and
27  see who's missing. You take the time to size up your class-
28  mates: who will be the friend, the enemy, the new love. You
29  catch up on the latest gossip: who got held back, who got
30  bumped up, who's been transferred. You get your assigned

1    seat and add that first line of graffiti to its freshly washed
2    surface. School reminds me of an old lady who's fixed her-
3    self up to go to the grocery store. She'll never look as good
4    as she used to, but that doesn't stop her from trying.
5        Yeah, I love the first day of school. It's the rest of the
6    year I hate!
7
8
9
10
11
12
13
14
15
16
17
18
19
20
21
22
23
24
25
26
27
28
29
30
31
32
33
34
35

# Pass the Peas, Please

1    *(Student trudges in and slumps down in a chair. There's a*
2    *pause.)* So, what are you in for? Skipping, huh? That's no big
3    deal. Mr. Adams calls you in and gives you a lecture about how
4    school is like your job and what would happen to your parents
5    if they skipped out of work? Then you get cafeteria duty for
6    two weeks which can be a pretty disgusting job, especially if
7    you're cleaning up after what happened today. *(Pause)* You
8    didn't hear? Oh yeah, you were here. Oh man, it was the food
9    fight to end all food fights. You should see the place — Dump-
10   ster City. They need to like bring in the city sanitation dudes
11   to hose down the place. One cafeteria lady even quit! Walked
12   right out in the middle of it. You could only tell she quit if you
13   were watching her mouth move 'cause it's not like anybody
14   could hear what she said. *(Pause)* Yeah, that's why I'm here.
15   There's a couple of other guys who should be here in a few
16   minutes. They sent me first. Got to get the ringleaders. Doesn't
17   that always make you think of a circus? *(Pause)* Me? No, but I
18   would love to take credit for starting it. It was amazing.
19   They'll be chiseling mashed potatoes off the ceiling when my
20   kids are old enough to go here. No, Danny did. Danny Bowen,
21   you know, big guy, thinks he's tough. Dark hair. Yeah, beat up
22   Tommy Adkins last year on the bus, that's him. He started it.
23       Danny and I have like this rivalry thing. If I run the mile
24   in seven minutes, Danny tries to do it in 6:50. That kind of
25   stuff. Well, today, if you got the hot lunch, you got shepherd's
26   pie. It's this hamburger, mashed potato glop with peas and
27   carrots. Really, it tastes better than it sounds. So Danny is like
28   picking out the peas so he can flick them up in the air and
29   catch them in his mouth. Well, I guess he flicks too hard and
30   all of a sudden I have smashed pea on my forehead. Yeah, he

1   still says it was an accident. Naturally, I gotta flick a piece
2   of carrot at him. It lands in his milk, a perfect shot. Then he
3   loads up with a spoonful of mashed potatoes, but I duck. He
4   ends up hitting Leroy in the back of the head. *(Pause)* I
5   know, can you believe it? Leroy, of all people. Well, Leroy
6   loses it. I mean, I've never seen anybody freak out like this.
7   He picks up his milk and chucks it at Danny. The milk box
8   hits the window behind Danny and explodes. Chocolate
9   milk goes everywhere. It was like some kind of signal.
10  Somebody yells, "Food Fight!" and it's a free-for-all. Peas,
11  carrots, mashed potatoes, a bag of Fritos, though I don't
12  know why anyone would waste a good bag of corn chips. I
13  guess they needed something to throw. Sandwiches, cottage
14  cheese, pizza. Whoosh, whoosh. Some kid decorates the
15  clock with peas and potatoes. Ketchup packs are squirting
16  everywhere. It looks like a war zone. Mr. Adams is blowing
17  his whistle, trying to get control and slips on a piece of
18  bologna. Boom! He's down! The cafeteria lady walks out.
19  Then it just dies down. One minute it's like a scene from
20  "Attack of the Killer Tomatoes" and the next minute, noth-
21  ing. Some girls were crying. A couple of kids got hurt, I
22  think. But you should see the place. Trashed! I can't imag-
23  ine what it's gonna smell like by seventh period. Man, you
24  should've been there. Oh yeah, I keep forgetting. You
25  skipped. Bummer, dude.
26
27
28
29
30
31
32
33
34
35

# The Carrot Express
## Is Comin' Your Way

1    *(Off-stage)* Hey, Bill! Aw, man, that was great. D'you see
2    Mr. A. bail on that bologna sandwich? Excellent! Yeah, man,
3    see you later. *(Walks On-stage and sits very properly in a chair.*
4    *There's a pause.)* Yes, sir. I would like a chance to explain my
5    side of the story. I see that William has already had a chance to
6    voice his side of this unfortunate incident and I'm sure that even
7    though he strongly believes that he is correct, I feel he's not
8    telling the absolute truth. Let me explain to you what really
9    happened in the cafeteria today.
10    I was enjoying a rather leisurely lunch with my friends.
11    The hard-working ladies who diligently serve us their gourmet
12    delicacies had made an exceptional shepherd's pie. I was espe-
13    cially enjoying the way they had browned the crust of the
14    mashed potatoes. Yes, sir. We had that cooking term in Home
15    Economics last semester so I am familiar with that particular
16    technique.
17    As I was saying, my comrades and I were deeply involved
18    in a discussion of which vegetable, when propelled, would have
19    the greatest velocity. I swore that the pea would be the no-con-
20    test winner due to its aerodynamic shape and size, but my
21    friend Brian argued that a slice of carrot would create more of
22    an impact due to its greater density. It seems to me that
23    William may have been eavesdropping which isn't very polite
24    if you ask me, because no sooner had Brian announced his
25    choice of vegetable than out of nowhere, plop! A carrot lands
26    kerplunk in my milk. I have to admit that it was a perfect shot.
27    Now that I have had a chance to think on it, perhaps I
28    should have turned the other cheek, so to speak, but at the
29    time, I felt retaliatory measures were in order. I'll admit it, sir.
30    I flung a pea at William. Yes, sir. I used the catapult method

1     which hit William right between the eyes. *(Points)* **Right here.**

2     **Needless to say, he was very surprised. I'm not sure he**

3     **expected that type of behavior out of me. I'm rather**

4     **shocked myself.**

5     **After that, I'm not sure what happened. I believe Leroy**

6     **thought we were aiming at him though I can't imagine why.**

7     **The next thing I know, he's hurling a chocolate milk at me.**

8     **Splat! It hit the window behind me and I'm now drenched**

9     **as you can see. I do remember hearing someone yell, "Food**

10    **Fight!" but I don't think I could identify that person. There**

11    **was a lot of noise.**

12    **And that's my side. I'm very sorry to have been**

13    **involved and next time, I'll go with my first instinct and**

14    **stay out of it. However, I do think that you should consider**

15    **that it was William who started it.** *(Pauses, then jumps out of*

16    *chair, losing the phony attitude.)* **What? You're giving me the**

17    **same punishment as Billy? Man, that's not fair. If I get sus-**

18    **pended one more time my stepdad says he's gonna send me**

19    **away to military school.** *(Slumps down in chair.)* **Aw, man.**

20    **This sucks. I may as well go home and start packing.** *(Stands*

21    *up.)* **So long, Mr. A. It's been nice knowing you. But hey,**

22    **look at it this way: every time you look at the clock in the**

23    **cafeteria you'll think of me. There's a pea at high noon!**

24

25

26

27

28

29

30

31

32

33

34

35

# All Together Now!

# The Brown Bag Blues

1     My mom makes the worst lunches in the whole world!
2     While the rest of the class is lip-smackin' their way through
3     pizza and chocolate chip cookies, I'm practically gagging
4     down my so-called "nutritious lunch." See, my mom is into
5     health food and since she's into it, our whole family has to be
6     into it, too. Not that everybody minds. My little brother was
7     probably a goat in another life, so he'll eat anything.
8     Every afternoon as I sit down to eat, I pray that inside that
9     brown bag is a bologna sandwich on white Wonder bread with
10     yellow mustard, a little snack cake thing individually
11     wrapped, and one of those juice boxes filled with some punchy
12     drink. Instead, what I usually have to look forward to is a
13     wholesome meal consisting of natural peanut butter on whole
14     wheat and zucchini bread that Mom makes in her bread
15     maker. The bread is real hard and dry and the peanut butter
16     makes wallpaper paste look appetizing. It's so dry I have to
17     wash it down with three milks. (I'm not allowed to have soda.
18     What a surprise.) If I'm lucky, Mom might put a granola bar
19     in the sack but most of the time, it's carrot sticks and an apple.
20     No one ever wants to trade lunches with me. I look like a dork
21     with all this healthy stuff. To make matters worse, I have this
22     teacher who makes sure we eat everything 'cause it's wasteful
23     to throw good food away. Some days I can sneak part of my
24     lunch into my book bag before she checks on us, but by the end
25     of the day, it smells like the dumpster behind the cafeteria. I
26     try to explain the situation to Mom, but she insists on feeding
27     me this crap. "You want to grow strong teeth and bones don't
28     you?" she'll ask. Believe me, I'd sacrifice my right arm and
29     my top row of teeth for an occasional bag of chips.
30

# School Lunches, or
## What You Don't Know May Kill You

1   Our school lunch menu is always the same. On Mondays,
2   we have hamburgers. Tuesday is mystery meatloaf day.
3   Wednesday is chicken pot pie. Thursday, macaroni and
4   cheese, and Fridays are, without fail, pizza. Most kids think
5   this is a great meal plan, but not the way our cafeteria makes
6   it. The hamburgers are these hard, flat, gray hockey pucks.
7   You need fourteen packets of ketchup to gag down the meatloaf
8   and the chicken pot pie usually has only one piece of chicken.
9   Once I got two pieces but that was in fourth grade. It's almost
10  always one. The mac and cheese is OK if you really like cheese,
11  but by Friday, that same cheese on the pizza is so greasy you
12  could lube your bike chains with it. Then it's right back to
13  hamburgers.
14      I didn't always have to eat school lunches. Back when
15  Mom and Dad were still together, Mom would pack me a
16  lunch after dinner made up of leftovers. Mom's a great cook so
17  I had these super deluxe lunches. All the other kids would beg
18  me to trade with them but I never would. Now Mom's never
19  home 'cause she has to work and when she is she doesn't feel
20  much like cooking. The other bad part about their divorce is
21  that we don't have enough money for everything, so now I'm
22  able to get the school lunches for free. My guidance counselor
23  told me that I was "really lucky" to be able to qualify for the
24  program. I don't think the guidance counselor has ever eaten
25  the lunch at our school. If I was really lucky, next Monday
26  would be lasagna!
27
28
29
30

# Firstborn

1     I'm the oldest of six kids and usually I don't mind, but
2     lately, being "head of the household" has become a real drag.
3     See, my Mom just had a new baby, so a lot of Mom's regular
4     chores have fallen on me. Make the bed. Do the laundry.
5     Watch your brother. Start dinner. Even if I wanted to do my
6     homework I wouldn't have time. My dad tries to help after he
7     gets home from work, but he usually falls asleep in front of the
8     TV after dinner. I guess he's really tired, but hey, so am I!
9     Once Dad's asleep, Mom starts in again. Watch your brother.
10    Empty the dishwasher. Feed the dog. Sheesh, sometimes I have
11    trouble remembering if I'm the son or the maid.
12       It wasn't always so bad. I remember when it was just Mom
13    and Dad and me. It's sort of fuzzy but things didn't seem so
14    rushed. Dad didn't just snooze and Mom didn't seem to
15    always be hurrying off somewhere. Then my brother was
16    born, and then my sister. Even after Kelly, I don't remember
17    minding it so much. I was older so I got to do stuff Kelly and
18    Richard couldn't do. I got to stay up late and watch the shows
19    that came on after the news. I got to ride the school bus to
20    school and they had to stay home. One time I got to go to
21    Grandma and Grandpa's by myself for the whole summer. I
22    got spoiled rotten. Gram made me all my favorite foods, I got
23    to sleep in my own room, and they took me toy shopping every
24    weekend so I could pick out something new. It was a blast.
25    When I came home loaded with toys, Mom and Dad dropped
26    the bomb on me. Mom was pregnant...again. This time with
27    twins. Double trouble. Grandma and Grandpa moved down
28    the street so going over to their house wasn't the special treat
29    I remembered. Actually, I think Gram spent more time at our
30    house helping Mom than at her own. One year after the twins,

1  and you guessed it, another baby. I don't know why they
2  keep having all these kids. They never seem to have time for
3  one of us let alone everyone. And private time, forget it.
4  Mom and Dad used to take us out on a special day all by
5  ourselves before we became an army. We'd go to the chil-
6  dren's museum or the circus and the rest of the gang had to
7  stay home with a baby-sitter. That was cool. Plus you got to
8  have Mom and Dad all to yourself. That never happens any-
9  more. No, when we go out, people stare and ask Mom, "Are
10  these all yours?" Like who else's would they be? One lady
11  even had the nerve to say something about how nice Mom
12  was for taking in "unwanted children" like we were strays
13  or something. Mom told the lady to mind her own business
14  and walked away.
15      Don't get me wrong. I love my brothers and sisters.
16  They are each really neat in their own way and most of the
17  time I don't mind helping out. That's what a family does:
18  helps each other out. I just wish someone would hurry up
19  and grow up so I could share the helping. It gets lonely at
20  the top.
21
22
23
24
25
26
27
28
29
30
31
32
33
34
35

# Bringing up the Rear

1      Being the baby of the family sucks! All my life I've been
2  stuck at the bottom. No matter how hard I try I will always be
3  the youngest. I used to think that if I could grow faster than
4  my brother or sister that I could be older than they were. It
5  was a big disappointment when I learned it just doesn't hap-
6  pen that way.

7      As far as I'm concerned, my brother and sister have it
8  made. My brother Derek is a senior. He has his own car and a
9  part-time job at Steak-n-Shake. He makes lots of tips because
10  all the girls think he's cute, so he always has a pocket full of
11  cash. Whenever he has a date or wants to get out of the house
12  all he has to do is say, "Bye, Mom. Be home later." If I tried
13  that I'd never get to walk out of the house again.

14      My sister Lauren has it pretty easy, too. She's a sophomore
15  this year and a cheerleader on the varsity squad. That means
16  on Friday nights she gets to go with the football team as they
17  travel around to different cities. Her boyfriend is the quarter-
18  back, so she always has a ride home after the game. Not that
19  they have to come directly home after the game. She has to be
20  in before midnight but only if it's a home game. If it's away,
21  it's whenever she gets home. Now that's freedom.

22      For me, it's a different story. My mom or dad has to know
23  exactly where I am every single second of every single day. If I
24  want to ride my bike to my friend's house, my mom has to
25  know which friend and what time I'll be home. I have to call
26  when I get there...etc. You'd think that I was in kindergarten.
27  I have to go to bed by nine-thirty on school nights and ten-thirty
28  on the weekends. Do you think my brother and sister have
29  bedtimes? Nooo!

30      On the flip side, they say I've got it easy. Me? Ha. Derek

1   says that Mom and Dad are much more lenient with me
2   than they were with either him or Lauren. I can't imagine
3   Mom and Dad acting stricter. Lauren says that when she
4   was in seventh grade, she had to go to bed by eight, not
5   nine-thirty. Yeah, and Dad walked three miles uphill in the
6   snow to get to school. I've heard that one, too! I may be the
7   baby, but I'm not stupid.
8
9
10
11
12
13
14
15
16
17
18
19
20
21
22
23
24
25
26
27
28
29
30
31
32
33
34
35

# Bookaholic

1     Hi. My name's Chris and I'm a bookaholic. I'll always
2 remember the first book I ever really loved, *Goodnight Moon*.
3 Now that I think about it, it's kind of a stupid book. I mean,
4 it's just this dumb bunny that won't go to sleep, so he says
5 goodnight to practically everything on the planet. Goodnight,
6 bed. Goodnight, rug. Goodnight, moon. Just go to sleep
7 already! But I remember liking it anyway. I liked the smell of
8 the pages. I even liked how the story never changed. You could
9 leave it on the bookshelf for five years and one day decide to
10 pick it up again and there would be that dumb, insomniac
11 bunny saying goodnight all over again.
12     Now I'm like this book addict. I just can't seem to get
13 enough. The local librarian knows me by my first name. She
14 sends me birthday and get-well-soon cards if she hasn't seen
15 me in a while. I've even had to replace my library card three
16 times, not because I lost them, but because I wore them out.
17 Every time I sit still for more than two minutes I start getting
18 this nervous itchy feeling like I've got to read something. I
19 read the backs of cereal boxes, billboards, catalogs, you name
20 it! *(Long pause)* I have even...um...on occasion...um...read
21 the bottom of the tissue box out of desperation when I'm...ya
22 know...doing my business in the bathroom. I know I have a
23 problem.
24     And bookstores. Don't even get me near a bookstore. One
25 time, my grandmother sent me fifty dollars for Christmas. I
26 was in the bookstore all day making my choices. Literally,
27 from ten am when they opened until five-thirty pm when I had
28 to go home for dinner. And guess what I bought? Nothing. Can
29 you believe it? Nothing. It wasn't that I didn't want anything
30 'cause I saw lots of books I liked and I even carried some

1   around for a while. The problem was, I couldn't decide.
2   Simply couldn't make up my mind. Reader's angst my
3   mom called it. That means I was suffering from indecision.
4   Downright weird.
5       But this reading isn't always a bad thing. Au contraire.
6   I've been able to use other people's words for my own devi-
7   ous purposes. Many a fair dame has succumbed to my
8   charms due to a well-written sonnet or poem borrowed
9   from one of the greats: Browning, Shakespeare, Silverstein.
10  Just slip the note into their algebra book with the message
11  "I thought of you when I read this…" and they stop you
12  between classes all glassy-eyed when the day before they
13  wouldn't have noticed you if you were drowning in quick-
14  sand at their feet.
15      On the other hand, I hate reading in school. The stuff
16  they make us read is so babyish. And you have to suffer
17  through "And Cherry…said to…Ponyboy, Hey, that's a stu-
18  pid name!…let's get…outta here." It's like being trapped in
19  Reading Hell.
20      Listen, I know I have a problem. That's why I came
21  here tonight. I really want to get better, but do I have to give
22  up *Goodnight Moon*?
23
24
25
26
27
28
29
30
31
32
33
34
35

# Math Maniac

1     *(Individual is facing Upstage talking to self as if pretending to*
2     *do an imaginary problem on the blackboard.)* **OK, let's see. You**
3     **have to carry the five and add three. Divide the remainder and**
4     **now convert to a decimal. Ta da!** *(Turns around to face audience*
5     *and bows.)* **I can't seem to get enough of math class. It's my**
6     **favorite subject without a doubt. It didn't used to be though.**
7     **Last year, I was a certified math retard. Honest! I could add**
8     **four plus seven and get twenty-eight which everyone should**
9     **know is not the correct answer. Heck, last year I wasn't even**
10    **smart enough to count on my fingers!**
11       **I think that I was math deficient at birth. My mom needs**
12    **a calculator to figure out how many kids she has** *(Holds up*
13    *three fingers)* **so I guess it's a genetic thing. Thank goodness my**
14    **dad has a vague idea about how to put numbers together or**
15    **else I would've failed math in every grade by now.** *(Pause)*
16    **Come to think of it, though, Dad could've been my problem.**
17    **Math always got horribly frustrating when Dad tried to**
18    **explain it. He'd take all this time sharpening my pencils,**
19    **adjusting the kitchen lights and rounding up enough paper to**
20    **build a gigantic fleet of airplanes. By the time he got around to**
21    **explaining the first problem, it was nearly bedtime. Each**
22    **problem had to be written out on its own piece of paper and**
23    **each step written clearly and legibly under the last step. With**
24    **all that preparation, I should be Einstein by now! It should**
25    **also go without saying that he never explained it the same way**
26    **as my teacher. He used some ancient method that he learned**
27    **one hundred years ago when he was in school. Too bad for me**
28    **that I live in the nineties. They teach Math different now. Dad**
29    **was very patient, but I just couldn't get it. I think I spent more**
30    **nights crying about math than I ever did crying about baby**

1   things as a baby.
2      But all that changed this year. This year I have Mr.
3   Wayne. When I'm in his class, it seems as if he is turning a
4   switch on in my brain. Everything is so easy. He explains
5   the problem step-by-step and BAM! An explosion goes off
6   in my head. The planets align, the angels sing and all is right
7   with the world. OK, maybe it's not quite that exciting, but
8   it's pretty close. I feel like a genius. So far my average is
9   110%. We get our report cards next week and I think I'm
10   gonna have my first math A ever. Math isn't quite as scary
11   now thanks to Mr. Wayne. Hmmm. I wonder how he is at
12   teaching spelling...
13
14
15
16
17
18
19
20
21
22
23
24
25
26
27
28
29
30
31
32
33
34
35

# You Know You Want Some

1    Psst, man. Come 'ere. Check this out. See what my brother
2  got for me? Cool, huh? What? Are you chicken? OK, baby,
3  fine with me. You're the one who's missing out. Run home to
4  Mama and tell. *(Pause)* Aw, who needs 'em.
5    It's all my brother's fault. He's the one who got me started.
6  Used to slip me some of my old man's beer after he fell asleep
7  during Monday night football. Ya know, if you drink enough of
8  it, it doesn't taste so bad. After awhile ya even learn to like it.
9    Then Gary moved to our school. He was so cool. I liked the
10  way the kids steered clear of him. He could walk down a
11  crowded hall and never get bumped. He made you respect him
12  or else. Gary could get you anything you wanted and he was
13  only a kid. He had connections. He used to know this homeless
14  guy that'd buy you anything if you gave him five bucks first.
15  Gary and I would sneak off into the woods behind school and
16  drink ourselves blind. Being drunk is just about the coolest
17  feeling there is. One minute you're feeling great and the next
18  minute you're falling down laughing at yourself. Ya know, if
19  you lie down on the ground and close your eyes, you can feel
20  the world spinning? It's like being on a ride at the fair. And
21  just like at the fair, after you get off the ride, you puke your
22  guts out. That's not so cool, but it does make you feel better.
23  You can only ride the Tilt-a-Whirl so many times.
24    Pretty soon, Gary and I discovered that we could bring
25  drinks to school if we just put it in our thermoses. We'd sit
26  around getting plowed at lunch and the stupid administrators
27  would think we were just cutting up. You'd never imagine how
28  much better English was once I started drinking. Mr. Driscoll
29  was almost bearable.
30    Then Gary got caught. Some cop saw the old bum give

1    Gary the bottle. His parents sent him away to one of those
2    help-my-drunk-son centers. Now Gary's a drag. He ignores
3    me in the halls and his parents won't even let me talk to him
4    on the phone. Drinking's more fun when you've got a buddy,
5    but even alone, school's never been such a blast. There's
6    this new guy who looks promising. I heard that he asked
7    some kid where he could get his hands on some drugs. The
8    kid shrugged but told him to ask me. Said I might know.
9    Cool. I've never touched the stuff, but how hard could it be
10    to get? Besides, I like having a reputation as a guy who can
11    get stuff. I like being able to walk down crowded halls and
12    not get bumped.
13
14
15
16
17
18
19
20
21
22
23
24
25
26
27
28
29
30
31
32
33
34
35

# A Spoonful of Welch's

1      Lots of kids think it's really cool to say they use drugs.
2  Take it from me, a lifelong user, I'd rather be uncool than
3  doped up. Cool is for ice cubes.
4      I'm a drug user, but it's not what you're thinking. I was a
5  really sickly baby. I was in and out of the hospital at least ten
6  times before I was two. Colic, pneumonia, jaundice — all
7  kinds of stuff. Then, when my parents thought they could
8  finally sleep through the night without making sure I was still
9  breathing, I got asthma. Heck, they were up twice as often
10  after that! I would wheeze and cough and gasp for air like
11  some giant fish and my parents would rush me back to the
12  hospital. The doctors and nurses would stick me with needles
13  and I'd have to sleep under an oxygen tent that night. After
14  several of these episodes, the doctor finally gave my parents
15  some pills for me to take whenever I had an attack. To me, that
16  pill was humongous. How was I supposed to gag it down? I'd
17  bite down and lock my lips together even though I was turning
18  blue. That pill was as fat as my finger! Mom and Dad would
19  frantically try to disguise it in peanut butter or Jell-O, but I'd
20  simply suck the stuff off, spit the pill out and wheeze away.
21  Then we'd make another trip back to the emergency room.
22  One nurse figured me out and emptied the capsule into a
23  spoonful of Welch's grape jelly. By the time I'd sucked the
24  jelly down, the medicinal beads were gone too.
25      Eventually, I did learn to swallow pills and it's a good thing,
26  too. I'm allergic to everything under the sun, so I have this vast
27  rainbow of stuff to swallow. When I hit puberty, I needed med-
28  ication for my cramps and PMS, (It figures.) So add that to my
29  already lengthy list of pharmaceuticals. I can't imagine the
30  number of teaspoons of jelly I'd be eating by now…

1    My friends constantly tease me about all my illnesses. I
2  keep a stock of drugs at each of their houses just in case.
3  They make fun of me whenever I return their clothes with
4  pockets full of used Kleenexes. For my birthday, they've
5  given me such entertaining gifts as a humidifier and a
6  porcelain pillbox. What do I look like? An old person? I'm
7  fourteen, not eighty-four. I like clothes too.
8    Recently, I've been diagnosed with diabetes, which has
9  given me a whole new section of my local pharmacy to dis-
10  cover. I've learned to jab myself in the leg with a needle and
11  test for high blood sugar. I should be a real hit at sleepovers.
12  Needle jabbing could be a real party pleaser.
13    So all you really cool drug users out there, take it from
14  an old pro — give it up. Why do something to make your-
15  self sicker when there are people like me who only want to
16  be well? I'd trade places with you any day. But no matter
17  what, I'm not giving up my addiction to Welch's grape jelly.
18
19
20
21
22
23
24
25
26
27
28
29
30
31
32
33
34
35

# Final Exam

1     *(Student is handed a folded test paper. Sneaks a peek between*
2     *the folds and clutches it to chest, turns the paper around to the*
3     *audience and shows it to them.)*
4     I am so brilliant. I am the smartest, brainiest person alive.
5     It's a wonder that I even allow the other people in my class to
6     get this close to my genius. I should seriously consider having
7     the teacher move me away from the rest of them so their stu-
8     pidness doesn't contaminate me. I got an A plus.
9     I'll have to admit, I was kinda worried about this test.
10     Final exam. It sounds so, so…final. Just one little screw-up
11     and wham! you have to repeat the whole grade all over again.
12     Same teachers, same textbooks, new kids. New little kids. All
13     your friends get to move on while you are held back, doomed
14     to hear Mr. Roberts tell the same corny jokes one more time.
15     Not that this has ever happened to me. Actually, I've even
16     skipped a grade. Went from second to fourth overnight. But
17     being held back is a different story.
18     School has always been easy for me. I don't even have to
19     study to get an A. I just read the book or listen to the teacher
20     explain the problem and I'm ready for the test. I see lots of
21     kids struggling with the easiest stuff. They look at me like I'm
22     a freak or something. Last year, this group of kids that hate me
23     'cause I'm so smart got together and told the teacher that I
24     cheated on a test. The teacher retested me all by myself with-
25     out any papers, books or anything. She even gave me the
26     pencil I used. And guess what? I got the same grade twice —
27     one hundred percent. The teacher apologized and the other
28     kids got detention for lying. It serves them right. Why should
29     I have to cheat? I'm naturally smart.
30     When the other kids aren't accusing me of cheating,

1    they're usually coming to me for help. I'm a whiz in science
2    and math. English is a little tougher 'cause it's mostly
3    creative writing, but I have a pretty good imagination so I
4    get by. Geography is just memorization and who can't
5    read? Plenty of people, I've been told. Mrs. Miller asked me
6    if I would be interested in being a part of a peer-tutoring
7    program called Pen Pals. It's where you teach another kid
8    the stuff you learned in class. Mrs. Miller said that some
9    kids learn better if they're not threatened by the subject
10   matter and when they see another kid can get it, they don't
11   feel so intimidated. I can't imagine being scared of reading,
12   but I said sure, I'd be glad to help. It's the least I can do.
13   Not everyone can be me!
14
15
16
17
18
19
20
21
22
23
24
25
26
27
28
29
30
31
32
33
34
35

# The F-Word... Failure

1    *(Student is handed a folded test paper, sneaks a peek between*
2    *the folds and promptly closes the paper back up again. Student*
3    *puts head down on the desk in despair.)*
4        I am so stupid. I am the stupidest person alive. It's a wonder
5    the other people in the class don't throw me out for being so
6    stupid and breathing stupid germs into the air. If I sat next to
7    me I would ask the teacher to move me far far away so my
8    stupidness wouldn't contaminate me. I got an F.
9        I wasn't always this dumb. Until this year, I was a fairly
10   decent student. Heck, last year I even got an award for being
11   the scholar of the week. My parents were so proud. They took
12   me to Burger King for my free dinner compliments of the
13   school. Then in the BK parking lot, my dad made a big deal of
14   putting the "My child was scholar of the week at Piney Grove
15   Elementary School" bumper sticker on the car. My mom even
16   took pictures of it. I think that's why it's so hard for them to
17   understand why I'm such a failure this year. "You're not try-
18   ing hard enough." "Put a little extra effort into it." "Honey, we
19   know you can do better. Weren't you scholar of the week?"
20   What if it was just a fluke, Mom? What if I'm really just a stu-
21   pid person disguised as a smart person and it just took twelve
22   years for the disguise to wear off?
23       In English we have all these papers to do. Algebra is so hard
24   I get a headache putting my name on the paper. We do such stu-
25   pid things in science that it's impossible to pay attention.
26        Who cares how many times the heads-up side of a coin will
27   come up when you flip it? Isn't it fifty-fifty? There are only
28   two sides to any coin, I know. Even I'm smart enough for that
29   one. Geography is a waste; worksheet after worksheet. I'm
30   never gonna move out of this country, so why should I have to

1 know what countries border Cambodia or Spain? And
2 reading…this sounds like it should be easy, right? You get a
3 book and you read it. Nope. That would be the farthest
4 thing from the truth. Reading uses all these scary terms like
5 "critical thinking skills and semantic mapping." Yikes!
6 We're in middle school, not college!
7       The worst part is when teachers hand back papers.
8 Some teachers hand back papers face up if they're good
9 and face down if they're bad. So what's the probability of
10 me getting a heads-up paper this year? One in one hundred.
11 Mr. Roberts, the science teacher, ranks your paper so if you
12 got a good grade you get yours back first. If you're a
13 dummy like me, you get it toward the end of the pile with
14 the rest of the losers.
15       I have only one ray of hope: Pen Pals. That's a tutoring
16 program after school in the media center where another kid
17 helps you out. It's my last chance or else. And when I say
18 "or else" I mean "or else Mom's threatening to pull me out
19 and home school me if my grades don't go up." As if I don't
20 feel stupid enough already. I'm not even capable of handling
21 a real education. My mommy will have to spoon feed it to
22 me just like when I was a baby. It's too bad we babies have
23 to grow up. Mom probably thought she was getting a real
24 winner when I was growing up. Now I'm just a dunce with
25 a faded scholar sticker.
26
27
28
29
30
31
32
33
34
35

# Psst, Number 4...

1     *(Talking very fast)* **Well, ya see, Mrs. Miller, it's like this:**

2     **when I came home from school yesterday I immediately sat**

3     **down to study for my vocab test because you've told us a mil-**

4     **lion times that prior preparation is the key to success. See?**

5     **And you thought I wasn't listening! So I sat down and opened**

6     **my book bag and my vocab workbook wasn't in there. I mean**

7     **it vanished! I was sure I put it in as I was talking to Heather,**

8     **but now that I think about it, I must have grabbed my science**

9     **notebook by mistake 'cause I had that and not my vocab book,**

10    **and since I didn't have a science quiz today what good was it?**

11    **So I went back outside and started to ride my bike back to**

12    **school to get the book 'cause I wanted to get a good grade and**

13    **all. On the way to school, I had to stop and move a turtle out**

14    **of the road so he wouldn't be roadkill or anything and then I**

15    **had to stop again 'cause he... (I guess it was a he but how can**

16    **you really tell with turtles?) he started back toward the road**

17    **again. By the time I got to school, all the gates were locked. I**

18    **started to panic 'cause I really needed to get that book so what**

19    **comes next I can only say was temporary insanity. I broke into**

20    **the school. Yes, I admit it sounds like I am lying. I mean, what**

21    **kid wants to break into the school? Break out, OK, I under-**

22    **stand that, but in, no way! Only I really did break in. Stop**

23    **looking at me like that! You can ask Mr. Watson, the security**

24    **guard, 'cause he caught me, and took me to his office and**

25    **called my parents to come get me. Boy, was my dad mad! You**

26    **should've seen him! I guess Mr. Watson interrupted him dur-**

27    **ing an important meeting. See, he's a lawyer and he was**

28    **probably, like, talking to some murderer or something. He**

29    **doesn't like to be interrupted when he's talking to clients. He**

30    **calls them clients even if they've murdered someone. Anyway,**

1    he had to leave work to come pick me up 'cause Mr. Watson
2    said I was breaking and entering and that really means
3    something to my dad, him being a lawyer and all. Honest,
4    all I really wanted to do was get my spelling book. Oh right,
5    vocab. Yeah, that's it. I just wanted to see if you were lis-
6    tening. So Dad and I go home and he gives me this really
7    long lecture about how disappointed he is in me and I
8    should've known better and didn't he and Mom try to teach
9    me right from wrong? I felt really bad even though I didn't
10   really do anything wrong. I was just trying to study. So we
11   get home and he says I have to stay in my room and think
12   about what I'd done. No TV, no stereo, no phone calls. They
13   said I couldn't even come down for dinner. Now I'm starv-
14   ing, I'm in trouble, and I still don't have my vocab book.
15   They didn't let me out until this morning. When I got to
16   school, Marc had left me a note in my locker that said he
17   borrowed my vocab book to study and would give it back
18   tomorrow, which is today. And that's why, Mrs. Miller, I
19   looked at Terri's paper during the test. *(Long pause)* You
20   were only going to congratulate me on my one hundred
21   percent? Uh-oh...
22
23
24
25
26
27
28
29
30
31
32
33
34
35

# I Shouldn't, I Couldn't, I Did...

1    Look, I'm telling you the truth. I have never done any-
2    thing like this before in my whole life. But you see, Toni is my
3    friend and it's really tough to say no to a friend, especially
4    when she's in trouble.

5    We've been friends for a really long time. She was the first
6    person I met when I started school here in third grade. We
7    like, clicked, ya know? We'd hang out after school and do
8    other stuff. We were on the same soccer team in the fifth
9    grade. We even had the same bus stop up until this year. This
10    year, Toni moved to an apartment across town. I don't get to
11    see her so much anymore. Mostly at school. But anyway, when
12    Toni moved away she like, changed. She started hanging out
13    with these really weird kids. These kids like hang out by the
14    boys' locker room and smoke and cuss and stuff. They get real
15    rowdy in the cafeteria and like, really trash the people who
16    walk by their table. Toni was never like that before. She was
17    always real nice to everybody. Now she is so mean. She told this
18    girl, Doreen, who has like really bad acne, that if she didn't get
19    those zits popped, no boy was ever gonna kiss her. Stuff like
20    that. I mean, she never would've said stuff like that before.

21    So now, like, today, she says, "Hey, Terri, what's the answer
22    to number four?" At first I tried to pretend that I didn't hear
23    her, but she kept whispering louder and louder. Like, I didn't
24    want Mrs. Miller to hear. Then I pretended that I didn't know
25    the answer, but she didn't buy that. I'm a whiz at English. It's
26    really easy for me. "OK," I said. Then when Mrs. Miller got up
27    to throw a piece of trash away, I leaned over so she could see
28    the answer for herself. I figured that if she, like, accidentally
29    saw it, it wouldn't really be my fault. Like, oops, instead of if
30    I told her the answer, that would be really be cheating. Well,

1   that's what I told myself anyway. Toni asked for numbers
2   six, nine and ten, too. Finally, I leaned down to tie my shoe.
3   Heck, if she was gonna keep bothering me she might as well
4   copy the whole darn thing! Then Mrs. Miller says, "Terri,
5   please guard your work." Like, now I'm in trouble and
6   Mrs. Miller is suspicious and I was just tying my shoe! After
7   class, when we were dismissed for lunch, I felt really sick.
8   Toni came up to me and told me that I was the best. Then
9   she walked off with her new friends. I've got one question:
10   If I'm the best, why do I feel like the worst?
11
12
13
14
15
16
17
18
19
20
21
22
23
24
25
26
27
28
29
30
31
32
33
34
35

# Paste, Crayons and Finger Paints

1　　　Of all the good things I have encountered so far in life,
2　nothing comes close to paste, crayons and finger paints. I love
3　the ooey-gooey feeling of paste, the fresh, waxy smell of new
4　crayons, and the thick slime of greasy paint. Oh sure, lots of
5　kids will tell you that an ice cream cone on a hot summer day
6　is the best, or the thrill you feel after you've managed to sneak
7　out and then successfully sneak back in is great. The really
8　bold ones who think they're mature will say sex even if they've
9　never done it before. Nope, all distant seconds. Paste, crayons
10　and finger paints are where it's at.
11　　　My obsession with childish things probably comes from
12　the fact that I never want to grow up. Ever. Peter Pan had the
13　right idea — stay young, play all day, and not have any cares
14　in the world. That's the life for me. Besides, who would want
15　to be a grown-up anyway?
16　　　If you're a grown-up, you have to get up extra early so you
17　can do a load of laundry before you have to drag your scream-
18　ing child out of bed. Then you have to put up with Junior's
19　pouty face 'cause you forgot to buy Crunchy Os at the store
20　and he has to eat Bran Bars instead. To make your morning
21　better the power company calls you to say they never got your
22　bill and you'll have to come down to the office before five
23　o'clock or they'll shut off your power. This means that you'll
24　have to leave work early and get docked half a day's pay. When
25　you finally get the whole mess straightened out, your son tells
26　you that he accidentally broke the neighbor's car window play-
27　ing Frisbee and she'll call you with an estimate. I know this is
28　how it is when you grow up 'cause this was my mom's life last
29　week. OK, so I was the pouty screaming kid, but like I said, I
30　don't want to grow up. I was just acting out  my part.

1     I use Mickey Mouse pencils and I carry a Hot Wheels
2    lunch box to school. It has this really cool thermos with a flip-
3    top straw. My friends say it's babyish, but I know they're just
4    wishing they had the nerve to carry that lunch box to school.
5    The cool thermos only comes with that lunch box.
6     A lot of my friends try to act grown-up and sophisticat-
7    ed at thirteen but I think it shows more maturity to do your
8    own thing and act ten! Little kids have more fun anyway.
9    Compare the playground noises of your average elementary
10   school playground with the noise on the PE field of any mid-
11   dle school. I ask you, who's having more fun? During PE I can
12   hear the little kids laughing and I wish I could just run down
13   the street and jump on a swing and push myself higher and
14   higher until my feet touch the clouds. I love the seesaw, too.
15   And that merry-go-round thing where you just spin and
16   spin and the world rushes past you in a blur and you can't
17   laugh because you lost your breath three spins ago. Then
18   our coach blows the whistle and it's time to go in the locker
19   room and listen to all the guys complain about how unfair
20   the teachers are and which girls are easy and how soon they
21   can get a license and drive away from it all.
22    Once I asked my mom if I could stay little and live with
23   her forever. She said that would be wonderful but that there
24   were too many exciting things she wanted me to discover as
25   I grew up. I was so depressed that I wanted to cry. To think
26   that one day, I wouldn't want to build a sandcastle or jump
27   on a trampoline makes me sad. But until then, I'm gonna
28   eat as much paste as I can so I can always remember the
29   three most important things: paste, crayons and finger
30   paints.
31
32
33
34
35

# Fourteen Going on Forty

1 Every once in a while I wish that I could just act my age.
2 It's just Mom and me at home, so I have a lot of responsibili-
3 ties most other kids don't. Normal kids go home after school,
4 put up their feet and watch TV until someone makes them din-
5 ner. Not me. When I get home from school I have plenty of
6 chores to do like mopping the kitchen floor, defrosting the
7 refrigerator, or starting supper. I usually have to run out to the
8 grocery store to shop for the evening's ingredients, but tonight
9 I think I have everything I need. Tuna casserole doesn't
10 require much. Once my chores are done I have to get my
11 homework finished right away 'cause as soon as Mom gets
12 home we eat and go right to our night job. She sings country at
13 this bar across town called Cowpokes and I bus tables. Legal-
14 ly, I'm not old enough to work at a bar, but Mom doesn't like
15 me to stay home at night by myself. We really need the extra
16 money so I have to go. She sings until one-thirty when the set
17 ends and then it's home to bed before I have to get up for
18 school again at six-thirty. It's a good thing I don't need much
19 sleep *(Yawns)* or else my life would be really awful.
20 Most nights I don't mind going to Cowpokes. The bar-
21 tender knows me and makes me virgin strawberry daiquiris on
22 the house. That means they're free. If it's a slow night, Juan,
23 the other guy that busses tables, and I play cards. He's teach-
24 ing me poker, which Mom isn't exactly thrilled about but since
25 we play with pennies she usually doesn't complain.
26 There was one time I got to waitress. What a disaster!
27 They were really busy, so they asked if I would help out. I had
28 just come back from a school dance, so I looked pretty old. Six-
29 teen at least. It was one of the rare occasions I got out of
30 cooking supper. Well, this young guy kept ordering drinks just

1   to have me bring them over. He was pretty cute and I guess
2   I was flirting with him, but all of a sudden he grabs me and
3   pulls me in his lap. I tried to laugh it off, but I was pretty
4   scared. My mom was in the middle of a song when she
5   noticed what he was doing. She stopped in the middle of the
6   song with the music still playing and screamed, "That's my
7   daughter. She's only fourteen." I could've died. Well, the
8   guy practically throws me off his lap and doesn't order
9   another drink for the rest of the night. The worst part is he
10  didn't even tip me!
11      That's the thing that gets me about my mom. Here I
12  have all these grown-up jobs like making supper and shop-
13  ping. And I practically live at a bar where I have a job until
14  one-thirty a.m., and she has a cow over the fact that I might
15  learn to gamble or date. Oh Mom, don't look now, but your
16  baby is fourteen going on forty!
17
18
19
20
21
22
23
24
25
26
27
28
29
30
31
32
33
34
35

# The Rumor Mill

1    Oh my God, come here, come here, come here! You're
2  never gonna believe what's happened. The eighth graders are
3  in such big trouble. Well, not like the whole grade, but a whole
4  mess of them. Didn't you see the police cars out in front?
5    OK, now I don't know all the details, but this is what I
6  heard. There's like this group of kids and I guess they've been
7  doing a lot of illegal things. Ya know, like breaking into peo-
8  ple's homes and getting into fights and stuff. Up until now,
9  nobody's known who they were. Well, last night, they really
10  did it. They broke into the school! I know, I know. It's like an
11  amazing feat but they really did. I guess they broke into the
12  main office last night. Ya wanna know why? This is so stupid.
13  They were changing their grades. Isn't that dumb? I mean,
14  why didn't they study in the first place? Duh! Well, while
15  they're busy trying to figure out how to turn on the main com-
16  puter, the silent alarm goes off. When the cops showed up, the
17  kids smashed one of the back windows and ran into the woods.
18  Haven't you seen all the glass? It's everywhere! They ran off
19  ,but they left the cops some big clues: their fingerprints and
20  Teddy Bresinski left his math homework behind. I told you
21  they were stupid. I guess he had written all his old grades and
22  course numbers on the paper. I bet he wishes now that he
23  would've forgotten to put his name on his paper. So the cops
24  are here questioning Teddy. I also hear that Mark Roberts was
25  another one of the kids, but I don't know who the rest were.
26    Can you believe something like this happened at our
27  school? It's so cool! I heard some of the teachers talking while
28  I was in the teacher's lounge delivering mail that they expect
29  Teddy and the other guys are gonna be expelled and that the
30  school is gonna press charges too. They are so far up a creek

1    without a paddle. I hope Teddy gets put in jail with a big,
2    hairy guy named Bubba. He deserves it. Teddy's a jerk.
3    Remember last year when he was going out with Christi and
4    she got in really big trouble 'cause like her parents came
5    home and caught them making out? Well, he was really two-
6    timing her 'cause I heard from Ashley that later that same
7    night he went over to Nicole's house to make himself feel
8    better, if you know what I mean. Guys like that deserve
9    Bubba.
10    *(Looks at watch.)* Oh my gosh, I gotta go. The bell's
11    gonna ring. Now, remember, this is just what I've heard,
12    but I did hear it from a really, really reliable source. Call me
13    later if you hear anything more. I still don't believe it. Noth-
14    ing so juicy ever happens here.
15
16
17
18
19
20
21
22
23
24
25
26
27
28
29
30
31
32
33
34
35

# The Wheel on the (Rumor) Mill Goes Round and Round...

1     Hey, you're not gonna believe what's going on! Yeah, this
2  big group of eighth graders is really gonna get it. They are in
3  such deep trouble. Haven't you heard? Hello, wake up in
4  there. Didn't you see the fleet of cop cars out in front of the
5  school? You didn't? Oh man, you must be blind. I even heard
6  that they're like calling in this special vice squad.
7     Now I've only heard bits and pieces from different people,
8  but this is the story I've been able to piece together. Teddy
9  Bresinski and Mark Roberts and a couple of other guys have
10  been on like this crime spree. Up until today, nobody knew
11  their identities. They just knew that some kids from this school
12  were going around totally trashing people's houses and starting
13  fights with other gangs. I even heard they robbed a convenience
14  store. Not like for money or anything serious, but just like ran
15  in and grabbed whatever they could and then ran out again.
16  Last night though, they hit the big time. Major felonies. They
17  broke into the school! Can you believe it? Why would anyone
18  want to break in here? It's not like it's a really cool theme park
19  or something. Well, anyway, they broke into the front office
20  and like trashed the place. They got into the main computer
21  since Mark is a computer whiz and all, and they changed a
22  bunch of stuff. No administrator is gonna be, like, able to do
23  any work for weeks 'cause the system is so screwed up. They
24  have to call in a professional computer geek to fix it. What
25  Teddy and the rest of the guys didn't know was that the office
26  is like rigged with a silent alarm. Is that cool or what? It's like
27  *Mission Impossible.* Well, the cops came and they shot out the
28  windows 'cause I guess they thought they were dealing with
29  pros. Haven't you seen the glass? It's everywhere!
30     Once the cops broke the glass, the guys figured it was, like,

1    time for them to be off like a prom dress and get outta there.
2    They ran off into the woods behind the school. The cops
3    swarmed over the school, but they were too fast for them.
4    Track team versus Donut Hounds? No contest! I heard they
5    had dogs and a helicopter looking for them but no luck.
6    Heck, they didn't need all that. Teddy left his math book
7    behind. It had a knife stuck in it and he had written a mes-
8    sage that said, "Die, teachers, die!" He tried to say
9    somebody took it out of his locker, but his fingerprints were
10   all over the office too. Once they got Teddy, he gave up the
11   others like that. *(Snaps fingers.)* Wouldn't you? If it was me,
12   I wouldn't go down alone. So like the cops are here now to
13   arrest them and haul them off to jail.
14       Oh wait, here they come now. *(Turns Stage Right)* Hey,
15   Teddy! What's the math homework for tonight? *(Cracks*
16   *up.)* Mark, man, I'd get yourself a soap-on-a-rope! Say hi to
17   Big Bubba for me, guys.
18       *(Turns back to audience.)* That was great! There's noth-
19   ing like working on a chain gang. The stylish clothes, the
20   male bonding, not to mention the leg irons. Yup, some of
21   High Grove Middle's finest, to be sure. I still can't believe
22   it. Nothing so juicy ever happens here!
23
24
25
26
27
28
29
30
31
32
33
34
35

# The Phone Call – Part I

1    Hi, is Heidi there? *(Pause)* Heidi, oh my God, you're not
2  gonna believe who said hi to me today in the cafeteria. It's
3  Leah, you dope, who did you think you were talking to? Any-
4  way, guess. Go on, guess. You'll never guess. *(Pause)* How did
5  you guess? Did you see us? Is he not, like, the best thing since
6  sliced peaches? I can't believe he goes to this school. It's like
7  he stepped out of the pages of HotTeen magazine. And he said
8  hi to me! Do you think he likes me? *(Pause)* What are you,
9  nuts? Of course I'm his type. I'm cute and I'm breathing,
10  aren't I? How do you know he likes that type of girl? Oh.
11  Heidi, would you be my very best friend and do me the most
12  humongous favor on the the planet? Don't say no right away!
13  Will you call him for me? Ya know, hint around. See if he
14  knows who I am. Find out if he's dating anyone right now.
15  *(Pause)* You will? When? OK. I'm sitting here by the phone.
16  I'm not gonna move one inch until you call me back so make it
17  snappy, OK? All right. See ya.
18    *(Hangs up the phone. Flips through magazine. Gets up and*
19  *begins to pace. Checks reflection in the mirror. Plays with her hair.*
20  *Checks figure. Becomes disgusted with reflection and runs back to*
21  *the phone.)*
22    Hi, Heidi. It's me again. *(Pause)* You were? Listen, did you
23  call him yet? I changed my mind. Don't call. I'm fat and ugly
24  and no guy in his right mind would want to be seen with me.
25  *(Pause)* You did? Oh no. Well? What'd he say? Did he say any-
26  thing good? Do I really want to hear this? *(Pause)* He does? He
27  isn't? Wow, that is so great. *(Pause)* Oh my god, he does? He
28  wants to sit with me at lunch tomorrow? Oh my god! Oh My
29  God! What am I going to wear? Will you sit with me? What
30  are we gonna talk about? Should I bring my lunch or should I

1  buy lunch? Don't laugh. This is a crucial decision. I mean,
2  like, what if I decide to buy my lunch and it's taco day. I
3  could spill it all down the front of whatever stunning outfit
4  I unearth from my closet or worse yet, the lunch gives me
5  taco breath! On the other hand, if I bring my lunch, will he
6  think the lunch is babyish? I mean, I'm not allowed to drink
7  soda so Mom packs me these juice boxes which I think are
8  pretty cool but he may not think so! Tell me. *(Pause)* OK,
9  I'll chance the school lunch. Heidi, you are the best friend
10 of all time. I can't believe I'm gonna have lunch tomorrow
11 with Alex Sanchez. *(Pause)* What's wrong? You called Alex
12 Mauro? That nose-picking computer geek? Well, call him
13 back! *(Pause)* What do you mean it's too late? Heidi, you
14 call him back or else I'm never speaking to you again!
15 *(Pause)* I know you are but what am I? Fine, be that way. I
16 hate you, too! *(Slams down phone. There's a long pause. Picks*
17 *up the phone again and dials.)*
18     Hello, Theresa. I have a really big favor to ask you. It's
19 Leah, you dope...
20
21
22
23
24
25
26
27
28
29
30
31
32
33
34
35

# The Phone Call – Part II

1    *(Phone rings.)* **Mom, I'll get it. Hello?** *(Pause)* **Yes, this is**
2    **Alex. Who's this?** *(Pause)* **Oh. We do? Oh, I never noticed you.**
3    **Sorry. Mrs. Miller makes me sit in the front of the room**
4    **because I have trouble seeing the board. I never really pay**
5    **attention to what goes on behind me. Usually it's just Josh and**
6    **Bobby and a bunch of other guys making fun of me. You don't**
7    **know the kind of abuse you get if you wear glasses and seem**
8    **to like school.**
9    *(Pause)* **Yeah, I think I know who she is, why?** *(Pause)* **She**
10   **does? No way! Oh man, that's so cool! The pages of HotTeen**
11   **magazine? Wow. My sister gets that magazine too. The guys in**
12   **there are like movie stars and everything. I can't believe she**
13   **said that. I had no idea I looked like that. What did you say she**
14   **looked like again?** *(Pause)* **Uh-huh. Uh-huh.** *(Pause)* **Is she**
15   **smart? I mean, no offense but I don't like stupid girls. It's OK**
16   **if she is, I mean, not everybody can be smart. I'm just saying**
17   **that I don't usually go for that type. Does she like computers?**
18   *(Pause)* **Well, a video game isn't exactly a computer but I guess**
19   **it'll do.** *(Pause)* **No, I'm not going out with anyone right now.**
20   *(Pause)* **Yeah, that's a good idea. I have lunch first rota-**
21   **tion. When does Leah?** *(Pause)* **She does? Great. Tell her I'll**
22   **meet her by the hot lunch line. I'll be sure to save her a place.**
23   *(Pause)* **OK. OK. Hey, thanks a lot for telling me. See you**
24   **tomorrow. Bye.**
25   *(Hangs up the phone. Flips through textbook. Gets up and*
26   *walks around. Checks reflection in mirror. He flexes his muscles*
27   *and poses. Smiles and winks at self. Sees imperfection and looks*
28   *closer. Becomes worried and then remembers something and looks*
29   *horrified. Runs back to phone.)*
30   **Hello, Justin? It's Alex. Oh man, you've got to help me.**

1  You know Leah in our English class? Dark hair, kinda
2  smart. *(Pause)* Yeah, I had no idea either. Yeah, she thinks I
3  look like one of the guys in HotTeen magazine. Don't laugh.
4  I don't think so either, but hey, girls are weird. Who knows
5  what they like? OK, so here's the problem. I'm supposed to
6  eat lunch with her tomorrow, but I always eat lunch with
7  Jenna. *(Pause)* I know that's a problem. That's what I just
8  told you. Will you sit with us tomorrow and act like Jenna
9  is with you? *(Pause)* Aw, come on. Who helped you with
10 your science fair project? Who helped you with Algebra last
11 night? Who covered for you when you broke your mother's
12 coffee table? *(Pause)* You will? Thanks man. You're the
13 best. Hey, buddy, I owe you one. Now make sure it looks
14 convincing. I'll just tell Leah that I had a good lunch, but I
15 don't want to get into a relationship right now. *(Pause)* I
16 know I am, but she doesn't need to know that! Or Jenna
17 either. Thanks again. See you tomorrow, bye.
18     *(To self)* Whew! That was a close one. Just one more
19 thing to take care of... *(Dials phone.)* Hi, is Mary Ellen
20 there? Hi, Mary Ellen, it's Alex. Did you understand the
21 math today? I'm stuck on problem fifteen and you're the
22 smartest girl I know...
23
24
25
26
27
28
29
30
31
32
33
34
35

# To Be or Not to Be

1     I can't believe it. I just can't believe it! This is incredible.
2  I did it on a dare. This is so great. Look at this cast list — I'm
3  the Wicked Witch of the West!
4     Bobby and I are in Mrs. Griffin's drama class. We like it a
5  lot because she always gives us parts where we cut up and fool
6  around. We have fun, make people laugh and get applause, not
7  to mention an A. I love it. Anyway, she announces to our class
8  that the school is gonna hold open auditions for *The Wizard of*
9  *Oz* and she'd like us all to try out since we're like in her class
10  and everything. We could pick which roles we wanted to audi-
11  tion for, but she wanted us there. Bobby and I just looked at
12  each other and smiled. Cool! We made a pact that he'd try out
13  for Dorothy and I'd try out for the Wicked Witch of the West.
14  Neither of us thought we'd get it, but it'd be so much fun
15  watching the faces of the judges as we tried out. Too bad we
16  couldn't watch each other. The auditions were gonna be held
17  in separate rooms.
18     I rented the movie to see what the Wicked Witch did. It
19  was pretty easy stuff. She laughed and bossed people around
20  and got to be really mean to Dorothy. I cracked up picturing
21  Bobby in that blue jumper dress thing.
22     The night of the auditions there were six girls and me.
23  Most of the girls sucked really bad. This one girl had the
24  wimpiest voice. She read the part where she tells Dorothy to
25  cough up the sparkly shoes. *(Imitates.)* Heck, who'd listen to
26  her? If I was Dorothy, I'd just push her out of my way and
27  keep on marching down the yellow brick road. There was this
28  one girl who was pretty good. She probably would have gotten
29  the part if I hadn't been there. She was real serious. You could
30  tell she had been practicing the part. The only thing is that the

1    witch in the movie wasn't dramatic serious, she was like
2    unbelievable serious. Like a cartoon character, not like a
3    real person. Oh well, I guess she missed that.
4        Well, the serious girl sits down and tells me to break a
5    leg. I just smiled. Boy, was she funny with all this serious
6    acting and drama lingo. The judges told me to do the part
7    where old Dot throws a bucket of water on Witchy-Poo. I
8    almost laughed out loud. It was perfect. I wished Bobby
9    could have seen me. I screamed and coughed and grabbed
10   my throat like I was choking. I staggered around the chorus
11   room grabbing at the piano and chairs for support. I almost
12   cracked myself up. I knew I was supposed to melt, so I
13   dropped down on my knees. I reached up like I was drown-
14   ing and yelled, "I'm going down for the last time!" It's not
15   even in the script! *(Laughs at self.)* I fell down on my stom-
16   ach and pretended to throw a tantrum, kicking my feet and
17   pounding the ground with my fist. Then I flipped over on
18   my back, screamed really loud, and went all limp and flop-
19   py. I was dead. Then I started twitching all over. Finally, I
20   put my arms and legs up in the air the way a mouse does
21   when it's dead and stiff. I wanted to hum "Taps," but I was
22   supposed to be dead, and as far as I know, the dead don't
23   hum. The judges and the other girls were all laughing. The
24   serious girl got up and left. I stood up and took a bow. I had
25   the best time. Now I get to do it for real! I only wish that
26   Bobby could be Dorothy. He doesn't care, though. He gets
27   to be a flying monkey, so he can act like his regular self. The
28   play's gonna be great. *(Pause)* I wonder what part the seri-
29   ous girl got?
30
31
32
33
34
35

# To Be or Not to Be

1    I can't believe it. I just can't believe it! Why does this
2  always happen to me? I studied and practiced. I practiced and
3  studied. Look at this cast list — I'm a flying monkey!
4    I was so excited when Mrs. Griffin announced the tryouts for
5  *The Wizard of Oz.* I figured all the girls would want to try out for
6  Dorothy 'cause that's like the lead and all. I suppose playing Glin-
7  da, the good witch, would be OK, but I was never big about
8  dressing up as pretty characters. For Halloween, I'm always a
9  ghost or a zombie or a devil or something just as evil. No, the part
10  I really wanted was the Wicked Witch of the West. For somebody
11  who likes scary stuff, this part would be a dream come true.
12    Auditions were planned for the following week. We
13  weren't allowed to see the scripts because it was going to be a
14  "cold read" (that means you're seeing your lines for the very
15  first time and you just have to try and act them as best you
16  can). So I went and got the library book instead. I even read
17  the whole thing though the witch isn't in all of the parts. I
18  wanted to get a good feel about what the other characters in
19  Oz thought of her. Ya know, their true feelings and reactions
20  and all. I memorized parts of the movie and practiced saying
21  them to my mom in my best witchy voice. *(Imitates Witch.)* "I'll
22  get you, my pretty, and your little dog, too!" The hardest part
23  was learning to cackle. *(Laughs evil witch laugh.)* Really, it's
24  harder than it looks. You should try it sometime. But by the
25  time auditions came, I felt pretty sure I could get the part.
26    Wicked Witch auditions were held in the chorus room.
27  There were seven of us. Just seven people out of the whole
28  school! Six girls and one...guy. Yeah right, I thought. Who's
29  gonna pick a guy for a girl's part? It's the Wicked *Witch* of the
30  West, not the Wicked Warlock. I still can't believe it.

113

1    Well, all of the girls basically sucked. This one girl had
2    the wimpiest voice. She read the part where the Witch tells
3    Dorothy to hand over the ruby slippers. *(Imitates.)* Heck,
4    who'd listen to her? If I were Dorothy I would just push her
5    aside and skip merrily down the yellow brick road.
6        When I was called, I felt pretty confident. I knew I was
7    better than the other girls, and like I said, who would pick
8    a guy for a girl's part? I got to read the part where the
9    Witch first meets Dorothy. *(Recites lines in best Witch voice.)*
10   I did everything I was supposed to: I looked up from my
11   script at the judges, I used my witch voice, I bent over and
12   hobbled around and I cackled really loud. The judges all
13   looked at each other, so I knew I was doing good. When I sat
14   down, the wimpy-voice girl said that I was really great and
15   she thought I would get the part. Then it was the guy's turn.
16   I even told him to break a leg when he got up to read. He just
17   smiled. He thought the whole thing was a joke. Some joke.
18       He was supposed to act out the part where Dorothy
19   throws water on the Witch and she melts. All he had to do
20   was scream and melt. There really weren't any lines. You
21   cannot imagine the scene that took place. I've never seen
22   anything like it in my life.
23       He screamed and coughed and choked. He clutched his
24   throat and staggered around the room grabbing at things.
25   When he got done destroying all the props, he fell to his
26   knees and reached up toward the sky with one hand. "I'm
27   going down for the last time!" he yelled. It's not even in the
28   script! He dropped down onto his stomach and kicked his
29   feet like he was throwing a tantrum. After that, he flips over
30   on his back, screams once more and goes limp. Then he
31   starts twitching. This wacko finally ends up with his legs in
32   the air like some giant cockroach. The judges started laugh-
33   ing and clapping. The other girls started cheering. I got up
34   and walked out. Needless to say, he got the part. I'm still
35   speechless and let's not forget...a flying monkey.

# I've Lost My Maternal Instinct. Have You Seen It?

1    Hello? Oh yes. Hi, Mrs. Mitchell. I remember you. You
2  do? Isn't that nice. Me? You want me to baby-sit your son?
3  Listen, Mrs. Mitchell, I think you've made a mistake. Trust
4  me. I'm the last person on the planet you want to watch your
5  kid. Really, he would be safer in the lion's cage at the zoo. I
6  know that I look like a perfectly responsible young woman,
7  and in a lot of ways, I am. But when I hear a baby crying for
8  longer than two seconds, something in me just snaps. My head
9  starts to spin around, my eyes roll back, and fire shoots out of
10  my mouth. I'm not a violent person and I'd never hurt anyone
11  so little and defenseless, but the sound of a baby screaming is
12  a lot like running your fingernails down a chalkboard.
13    My friends all think babies are cute, adorable, precious.
14  You should call one of them. They ooh and aah over this little
15  someone with spit dribbling down its chin. If someone older
16  did it, they would think it's gross. To me, spit's gross at any
17  age. They talk in these ooey-gooey voices that they would
18  never use at any other time in their lives. They sound like
19  they've just arrived from another planet. You'll never catch
20  me talking like that.
21    The trouble with babies is that they are so little. Their
22  shoes can fit in the palm of my hand. I'm sure that I would
23  break him. Once I was in the glassware department with my
24  mom and she asked me to put back one glass. Just one. Just set
25  it down and walk away. No, no. I set the glass down and it
26  knocks the one next to it down so I fumbled to catch it and
27  wound up knocking down the whole shelf and everything
28  underneath it for good measure. It cost $479.43 to replace.
29  Mom says I'm not allowed to go in the glassware department
30  again until I'm seventy-five years old. Heck, by then I won't

1    be able to see what glasses I'm buying anyway.
2        Babies stink and they're messy. The food is messy going
3    in and it's worse coming out. Remember the incident with
4    the glasses? Don't even think about what I could do with a
5    dirty diaper! Really, I'd be the worst baby-sitter ever. No,
6    don't give me that look. It's not an excuse. Really, I hate
7    kids. *(Notices baby for the first time.)* Hey, hi there, little guy.
8    Aren't you a big boy? What's this on your tummy-wummy?
9    *(Pause)* Well, maybe this once it wouldn't be so bad. But
10   I'm definitely not reading bedtime stories. *(Walking Off-*
11   *stage, turns back to the audience)* Well, maybe just one...
12
13
14
15
16
17
18
19
20
21
22
23
24
25
26
27
28
29
30
31
32
33
34
35

# Oh Boy, Babies!

1   I go for younger chicks. Not just a few years younger like
2 in sixth grade or something, but still in diapers younger. Real-
3 ly, I'm not a pervert or anything. I just love babies.
4   I'm an only child, so I never had the chance to be the older
5 brother. I think I would've been a great big brother. Lots of
6 other guys dream about movie stars or supermodels, but I have,
7 like, this daydream where I take my little brother or sister to
8 the park. It's a clear day, cool but not cold. I make sure the
9 little tyke is all bundled up just in case he gets a chill. I show
10 them how to go down the slide. I push them really high on the
11 swings and I lift them up to get a drink at the water fountain.
12 All the other kids ask if I'm the big brother and I proudly say
13 yes!
14   My friend Jimmy says it doesn't happen like that. Jimmy
15 has three younger sisters and he wishes he were me almost
16 every day. His mom is always asking him to change the baby
17 or help Lily get dressed or check Angie's homework. Some-
18 times, he's more like a parent to them than his parents. He
19 hates it. He loves his sisters but once in a while he would like
20 to ride his bike to my house without Angie following him. I
21 think he's the luckiest kid in the world. That's why I like baby-
22 sitting. It gives me a chance to take care of littler kids.
23   Baby-sitting is the best way I can think of for a kid to earn
24 money. Who would want to get all hot and sweaty mowing
25 lawns when you can be running through a sprinkler with a
26 two-year-old? Most of the kids I baby-sit have great toys to
27 play with. Sometimes I don't know who's having more fun, me
28 or the baby! But it's not all fun and games. Baby-sitting is a
29 big responsibility too.
30   Last year before my parents would let me baby-sit, I had

1    to take this class at the YMCA. See, it was a baby-sitting
2    course and they taught us all kinds of stuff that you need to
3    know if you're baby-sitting. Most of the stuff I already
4    knew, like how to change a diaper or call 911 if there's an
5    emergency. I've had a lot of practice thanks to Jimmy's
6    mom. But they also taught us stuff I didn't know like how
7    to bathe babies. We didn't use real babies, but I wish we
8    would've. I felt really stupid giving this big, floppy doll a
9    bath. It was good information for future use. Since then,
10    I've gotten to give baths to lots of slippery, wet kids. Yester-
11    day, my mom took me to the Y again to register for a new
12    class — CPR. She said it would be a smart thing to do
13    'cause parents would feel more comfortable leaving a small
14    baby with me if I knew more advanced emergency proce-
15    dures than just dialing 911.
16        I can't wait to learn 'cause it's really important to
17    know. Like this one time, Jimmy's little sister, Lily, fell in
18    their pool. She could swim, but I guess she just got scared
19    'cause she just started screaming anyway. Angie and Jimmy
20    and I all ran outside. I was about to jump in, but Jimmy just
21    threw her a life preserver and pulled her into the shallow
22    end. It was hanging there all the time and I never even
23    noticed. Like I said, Jimmy is responsible and a lot like a
24    parent. He thinks about things first and doesn't react on
25    impulse. That's very important when you're dealing with
26    little kids. It's scary to think about what could've happened
27    to Lily if Jimmy hadn't been there. I hope that if I'm in that
28    kind of situation again, I'll do the right thing...like Jimmy.
29
30
31
32
33
34
35

# I'm a Virgin, So Sue Me!

1    The other night when Mom and Dad were at the movies,
2  Teddy came over. *(Repeats slowly to self.)* Teddy came... Oh my
3  God! *(Giggles nervously.)* Yeah, well...um, see we were up in
4  the rec room and we were just watching this dumb made-for-
5  TV-movie. He had his arm around me and uh...you know...he
6  was trying to feel my...I mean, like, I didn't know what  was
7  going on, duh! So, I said, "Stop Teddy," and he goes, "What?"
8  like he doesn't know what's going on. Double duh! We go back
9  to watching the movie and he goes back to trying to feel my...
10 ya know. So this time I let him. First he was just brushing his
11 fingers against my shirt. I looked at him out of the corner of
12 my eye and he just pretended to watch the stupid movie. Can
13 you believe it? My stomach was doing flip-flops. But then he
14 starts grabbing it, really tugging on it. Tugging, I know. Like
15 it would come off or something. He looks at me and his eyes
16 are all glassy like a big ol' fish. So I said, "What's wrong with
17 you?" And he goes, "What?" and then he starts kissing me.
18 He's a real slobbery kisser when he's all hot. Like in school it's
19 a quick peck, but that night it was all sloppy and wet. Then,
20 this is the best part, he says... Oh my God... OK, I'll just say
21 it quick. He says, "Put your hand here," and he starts to take
22 my hand and pull it towards his you-know-what! Oh my God,
23 I freaked! I screamed, I think. Then my parents came home
24 and we both got in major trouble 'cause I'm not supposed to
25 have a boy over if Mom and Dad aren't home. So like, I'm
26 grounded for a thousand years and I can't call Teddy any-
27 more. Like I could if I wanted. Teddy won't even speak to me.
28 I'm a virgin, so sue me!
29
30

# My Arm Fell Asleep – Really!

1    It was the worst, man. The worst! I am never going out with
2    Christi again! See, we were up in her rec room Saturday night
3    watching TV and all of a sudden she goes, "Teddy, hold me."
4    Real dramatic like, like she's been reading too many love stories
5    or something. So I put my arm around her 'cause she does smell
6    nice and close is a good thing. After a while I couldn't feel my
7    fingers 'cause my arm was so numb. I didn't want to move it
8    'cause I didn't want to bother her and I liked having her so
9    close to me. I was just trying to get circulation going by wig-
10   gling my fingers and she says, "Teddy, stop." I didn't even
11   know that I did anything! We go back to watching the movie
12   and she leans forward to stretch and there's her...ya know...
13   in my hand. Boy, you can't imagine how fast the feeling came
14   back into my arm. I figured that if she wanted her...ya know
15   ...in my hand, who was I to say no! It was more than she ever
16   let me do in school. I went out with her for three whole weeks
17   before she let me kiss her. Well, I pretended to watch the
18   movie, but I couldn't tell you what happened. I had my mind
19   on other things, if you know what I mean. I was getting pretty
20   cranked up, so we started kissing. I was kinda uncomfortable
21   with my arm around her and her arms all bunched up between
22   us so I said, "Put your arm here." Ya know, like, around me?
23   *(Demonstrating)* Honestly, that's all I said. She goes nuts. She
24   starts screaming and jumps away from me like I'm attacking
25   her and she was the one who started it all! Then her parents
26   come home while she's screaming and we get this big lecture
27   about being unsupervised and that it's for our own good and I
28   remember when I was your age kinda stuff. She's grounded
29   for the rest of the semester and can't talk on the phone or see
30   me or anything. Like I would want to! Who wants to be seen

1    **with a girl who freaks out when your arm falls asleep!**
2
3
4
5
6
7
8
9
10
11
12
13
14
15
16
17
18
19
20
21
22
23
24
25
26
27
28
29
30
31
32
33
34
35

# The Baker's Dozen (& Then Some)

1      OK, that's it! I've had it. No one else in my family is
2  allowed to get married, remarried, divorced, separated, date
3  or otherwise until I decide to be a grown-up. I've got way too
4  many parents.
5      I started out just like everyone else. Two parents. Count
6  'em, two. A mom and a dad. Well, my dad ran off when my
7  mom got pregnant (they were just kids anyhow) and then I
8  was down to one. One parent. I envy those single parent kids
9  now...
10     When I was two, my mom got married to my dad. I call
11  him "Dad" 'cause he's the only dad I can remember. He's a
12  great guy and I love him a lot. I've even got his last name. We
13  do all sorts of cool stuff together and have a great time. He and
14  Mom were together for ten years. Last year was the tenth year
15  and it wasn't pretty. Mom and Dad would hardly talk to each
16  other. In a way, I wish there would've been a lot of fighting. At
17  least there would've been noise. Instead, they'd go for days
18  without talking at all. They'd send messages through me: "Tell
19  your father this," or "Give your mother that." It was awful.
20  When they finally split up, everyone was happier. Dad and
21  Mom both have custody of me so I still get to see everyone.
22  Unlike some kids, I don't mind the arrangement. Then this
23  year, Dad got remarried. Shortly after, so did Mom. Now keep
24  track. This is where it gets confusing. Two parents plus two
25  grandparents per parent is six plus two step-parents plus their
26  two parents each is twelve. Got that?
27     It took some adjusting, but I eventually got everyone's
28  name right. Fortunately, I like all my parents, step, adopted or
29  otherwise, so this makes it a little easier. Now, get this. Just last
30  night my real dad, the guy that ran off on my mom, called my

1 real mom to say that he's gotten his act together, he's mar-
2 ried (great), has two kids, blah, blah, blah, and wants to get
3 to know me so we can all be a family. Hey, mister. I've
4 already got enough family to populate a small country.
5 What makes you think I want to add yours? Mom said that
6 it sounded like he's really changed and that I should at least
7 give it a chance. I don't see why. This weekend, while all my
8 friends are having a blast with their one or two parents, I'm
9 gonna have to add another two to my collection. Twelve
10 adult parents or grandparents plus two new parents (one
11 real and one step) plus four additional grandparents equals
12 eighteen. Divided by one, me! I don't even want to think
13 where I'll end up for Christmas. All right people, enough is
14 enough.
15
16
17
18
19
20
21
22
23
24
25
26
27
28
29
30
31
32
33
34
35

# On My Own

1    *(Student is flipping through a collection of loose photos.*
2    *Finally, selects one and studies it closely. After a moment, he/she*
3    *holds it up for the audience to see.)*
4    This is a picture of my real mom and dad. My foster par-
5    ents don't know I have it or else they'd probably be mad.
6    "Why would you want to remind yourself of those people? Put
7    the past behind you. Think about your future. Let me give you
8    a hug." My foster parents are big on hugs. *(Pause)* I guess I
9    keep this picture to remind myself that even your parents can
10   turn on you and treat you bad. You can't trust anyone but
11   yourself.
12    Our life together was always weird. My mom and dad didn't
13   exactly hold nine to five jobs. "We do what we have to do to get
14   by..." They were free spirits, I guess, and moved around a lot.
15   Once they even worked the carnival circuit. Dad ran the Tilt-
16   a-Whirl and Mom sold cotton candy and stuff. Not that I could
17   ever tell anyone at school. Nobody's parents at High Grove
18   Middle have that kind of job. All their parents are doctors and
19   lawyers and Indian chiefs. Compared to them, my parents
20   are trash.
21    Well, we moved around a lot but things were basically OK.
22   I had food, clothes to wear, and even some toys. I think my
23   parents weren't into being parents. They made me call them
24   by their first names like we were all just friends living togeth-
25   er. By the time I was ten, I had been to fifteen different schools.
26   That's where the trouble started. I had just started a new
27   school and Dad was working construction. Then he got hurt.
28   Fell off some scaffolding 'cause he was drinking during lunch.
29   Broke a bunch of bones and because he was drinking the com-
30   pany said they didn't have to pay any Workman's Comp. That

1   was fine with Dad. He just started staying home and drink-
2   ing, collecting his unemployment. He got real mean and
3   that's when he started slapping Mom and me around. One
4   night, Mom just got up and left. No note. Nothing. Just
5   poof!...and she was gone. Sometimes when Dad's bottle ran
6   dry I would remind him that we needed to buy food. He'd
7   give me twenty bucks. Boy, you should see how far I could
8   stretch twenty bucks! I could eat for weeks.
9       My teachers started getting all suspicious and asking
10  me questions like what my parents did and what I had for
11  dinner last night. I told 'em my dad was a police officer who
12  worked the late shift and my mom was a waitress. I said I
13  got to eat whatever I wanted at the restaurant and last night
14  I had pork chops with mashed potatoes and cherry pie
15  when really all I had was a bag of Cheetos. Some lady from
16  the school came out to our trailer and told Dad that they
17  were concerned about me and was everything OK? Dad
18  beat the crap out of me for not being more careful. The next
19  day, the teacher figured out that my fat lip didn't come
20  from tripping on a crack in the sidewalk. "Did your daddy
21  beat you?" she asked. "He's not my dad," I told her. "His
22  name is Fred. Just Fred." From that day on, I didn't think
23  of them as my parents any longer. They're just Fred and
24  Jean. See, parents don't slap you around or run out on you.
25  Parents don't forget to feed you or kiss you goodnight.
26      Yeah, I guess I keep this picture so I can keep the dif-
27  ference straight in my mind. Parents are the people who
28  love you while the Freds and Jeans of this world could sim-
29  ply care less.
30
31
32
33
34
35

# Respect Your Elders

1      When I was little, my family moved around a lot 'cause my
2  dad was in the Army. We lived in a lot of places and met a lot
3  of people. It was pretty neat. Because we moved so much, I
4  didn't start kindergarten until I was six. I didn't much care.
5  Six is pretty much the same as five except I was bigger. Then
6  while I was in the fifth grade, we moved three times. My teach-
7  ers agreed that it was probably a good idea to repeat the grade
8  since I'd missed so much. My parents agreed that it was prob-
9  ably a good idea to repeat the grade since I'd missed so much.
10  I, for the record, did not agree. I'd learned enough. When Sep-
11  tember came around, there I was with a new group of former
12  fourth grade babies learning all the stuff I'd gotten in bits and
13  pieces all over again. Dad left the military shortly after so we
14  haven't moved in a while. Lucky me. I'm still stuck with the
15  toddlers one grade lower than I should be.
16      It's not like I'm a dumb kid. I get good grades, especially
17  since we're not moving around all the time. After I got all A's
18  the entire year, I begged and pleaded to be moved back up to
19  the grade I was supposed to be in. My teachers decided that
20  since I had done so well that I was probably in the perfect
21  grade for me. My parents decided that since I had done so well
22  that I was probably in the perfect grade for me. Again, let the
23  record reflect that I wholeheartedly did not agree. When Sep-
24  tember came around, I was still stuck with the same twirpy
25  little kids. That was three years ago. Now I'm the oldest per-
26  son in my class, on my team and probably in the whole school.
27  I'm fifteen and a half. I'll be sixteen by the time school lets out
28  in June.
29      I'm the only kid I know of with my driver's permit. All of
30  the other parents stare when Dad drops me off at school. They

1    must figure that I'm in high school until I get out of the dri-
2    ver's side and Dad drives away.
3        All of my friends go to the high school. They hassle me a
4    lot for being a baby in middle school. Kelly, this girl I really
5    like, is only fourteen and a half and she's in ninth grade. I
6    heard she wouldn't even consider going out with me until I
7    got into high school. I'm older than she is but I'm still in
8    middle school? Something's wrong here.
9        The kids at my school are pretty nice, but we don't have
10   much in common besides what's for homework. One of the
11   girls in my class found out that I hang out with a bunch of
12   juniors and seniors. Well, the blabbermouth told her
13   friends and the teacher overheard who told the guidance
14   counselor who called my mom to let her know she was con-
15   cerned about the company I was keeping. Mom had to
16   explain that I wasn't some little kid. Heck, in a couple of
17   months, I'll be driving to my after-school job. That nosy, lit-
18   tle girl should really learn to respect her elders!
19
20
21
22
23
24
25
26
27
28
29
30
31
32
33
34
35

# Baby Me!

1    Everywhere I go, I'm always the baby. I'm the baby at
2  home and I'm the baby at school. Being the baby at home is
3  OK 'cause the babies get special privileges. My brothers are
4  way older than I am and most of them are in college, so I basi-
5  cally have my parents all to myself. I was their late in life
6  surprise. Besides, I'm the only girl in my family. Girl babies
7  always get more stuff. I'm spoiled rotten.
8      At school, being the baby is a different story. When some
9  of the kids found out I was only eleven and in the eighth grade,
10  I got hassled really bad. They started calling me Einstein and
11  sticking brain stickers on my locker. My parents didn't think
12  it was so terrible to be called smart, but I didn't tell them that
13  they also said I still played with my Barbies at home. (OK, so
14  this is true. Still, no one wants that kind of thing blabbed all
15  over school.) No one wanted to be friends with me. Ya know
16  what I did? I gave myself a birthday party. Yup, six months
17  before I was supposed to turn twelve, I made myself thirteen.
18  When the kids said, "I heard you were only eleven," I'd say,
19  "Yeah, two years ago. You shouldn't believe rumors." After
20  that, everyone started treating me fine. I can't believe how
21  hung up on numbers some people are…
22      Still, my age causes me problems. I can't get into PG-13
23  movies without an adult. I'm a heck of a lot shorter than most
24  people at "thirteen." And though I might be able to convince
25  people my age is thirteen, I think my body got lost somewhere
26  around ten! The blackboard at school has more curves if you
27  know what I mean. I have no hips to speak of, and there isn't
28  a boy in my class who's looking at these pencil posts I've got
29  for legs. Most of the girls in my class have the bodies of some
30  high school prom queen even if their brains are definitely

1   stuck in middle school. I don't blend in anywhere.
2      When I go home at night, I'm so glad I can stop pre-
3   tending to be older. Mom and Dad just want me to be me,
4   no matter what age I am. And if that means I need to restyle
5   my Barbies' hair before dinner, then so be it!
6
7
8
9
10
11
12
13
14
15
16
17
18
19
20
21
22
23
24
25
26
27
28
29
30
31
32
33
34
35

# Spend a Little, Save a Lot!

1     My parents call me a pack rat, but I prefer the term "col-
2  lector." I can't help it if I see treasure where other people see
3  trash. It's truly a gift. If hoarding is a habit, then I've made it
4  an art form.
5     I save everything, and I do mean *everything*. I have every
6  old homework paper I've ever turned in, every note received
7  from a friend, birthday cards, Valentines, you name it. Mom
8  says it's a fire hazard, but who knows when you'll need to
9  prove something. I just want to be prepared.
10    I've saved all my toys since I was a baby. I think Mom may
11  have given some away when I wasn't big enough to know the
12  difference, but ever since I learned the power of the word
13  "Mine!" I've kept them. Once I tried boxing up a few games
14  that I hardly ever play. Wouldn't you know it, the next day
15  when Paula came over, she asked if I had it. After that, I
16  learned to keep everything where I can see it.
17    You should see my room! Most "collectors" are rather
18  messy but I, on the other hand, am excruciatingly organized.
19  Listen, with this much stuff, you've got to have a system.
20  Everything is sorted by size, shape or function. I have boxes all
21  labeled with their exact contents. My stuffed animals sit lined
22  up on shelves. Since I've naturally saved lots of clothes, the
23  ones I wear most go on top and the ones I can't bear to throw
24  out go on the bottom. The government should hire me to get its
25  act together!
26    Though I collect a wide variety of stuff, the one thing that
27  I'm absolutely brilliant at saving is money. Compared to most
28  kids my age, I'm loaded. Money's no different than anything
29  else I collect. If I don't save it, I may need it later and then I'm
30  really screwed. I always take the time to pick up change from

1   the sidewalk. I've got this empty water jug filled with coins.
2   I've had to empty it three times so far in my life. Each time
3   Mom and I have taken it to the bank, there's been close to
4   five hundred dollars in it. You do the math. When I was lit-
5   tle, my mom caught me trying to fill up my pockets with the
6   quarters that had been tossed in a public fountain. It nearly
7   killed me to throw them back. After all, what good were
8   they just sitting there?
9      And it's not just my money that I'm good at saving. I've
10  saved my parents a bundle too. I won't let Mom buy clothes
11  for me unless they are on sale. (It makes me sick to think of
12  the mark-up.) I always insist that she buy the generic
13  brands when we're in the grocery store and I'm shameless
14  at bargaining. Last year, when our refrigerator died, my
15  parents took me with them when they went to buy a new
16  one. All the salespeople thought it was really funny to see a
17  kid trying to talk the price down. Funny or not, I still saved
18  my parents three hundred bucks.
19      Mom and Dad are really proud that I've learned such
20  an important skill so early on in life, but I get the feeling
21  that just once, when they ask me what I want for Christmas,
22  they'd rather have me say a new bike or the latest "Loud
23  Guys" CD instead of "just money." Believe me, this year
24  I'm really gonna try to please them, but I'll only agree to a
25  new bike if they get it at half price.
26
27
28
29
30
31
32
33
34
35

# There's a Hole in My Pocket

1      *(Student is frantically searching the stage area for "money."*
2  *Every few moments, he should bend over and pick up something*
3  *and put it in hand or pocket.)*
4      **Aha! Finally!** *(Counting imaginary coins)* **All right!** *(To self)*
5  **I've got just enough money for a pack of Super Bubble Gum.**
6      *(To audience)* **I never have any money. Zip, zilch, nada. I'm**
7  **constantly broke. My friends don't even ask me to borrow fifty**
8  **cents for a soda or a quarter to make a phone call home. It's a**
9  **well-known fact that I am without fundage. I must have, like,**
10  **this hole in my pocket. Money just seems to find its way out of**
11  **my hands.**
12      **Once my mom gave me fifty dollars and a list to go grocery**
13  **shopping. Wow, fifty dollars, I thought. I've very rarely seen**
14  **fifty dollars let alone held it in my hand. On my way to the**
15  **store, I passed a convenience store. Since it was summer and**
16  **really hot, I thought Mom wouldn't mind if I bought myself a**
17  **cherry slush. Mom would have known to give me extra money,**
18  **wouldn't she? No one ever spends exactly fifty dollars at the**
19  **grocery store. Well, once I got the slush, I decided that I was**
20  **kinda hungry, too, so I grabbed a bag of chips. And hey, when**
21  **did this new issue of Teenage Avenger come out, and oh, look,**
22  **I'll get Mom some fresh flowers. She loves fresh flowers. But**
23  **honest, that's all I got!**
24      **When I got to the grocery store, the girl scouts were hav-**
25  **ing a white elephant sale in the store parking lot. There was**
26  **this really cool, old lamp that I knew would look great in my**
27  **room. Besides, it was only ten dollars. The girl scouts is a good**
28  **cause, isn't it? While I was paying for the lamp, I saw a pair of**
29  **salt and pepper shakers shaped like people bending over. One**
30  **was a boy in overalls and the other was a girl 'cause you could**

1    see her ruffled panties. They were only two dollars, so I got
2    those for Mom too. She'd think they were funny. It was
3    hard to manage 'cause I had so much extra stuff to carry,
4    but I finally got all the things on Mom's list. When the
5    checkout girl rang up the total, it came to $48.72. Needless
6    to say, I had to put a few things back.

7        When I got home, I gave Mom her prizes for being such
8    a great mother and told her how much I loved her. Then I
9    made a quick exit to my room. Mom came up a few minutes
10    later to ask where the rest of the groceries were. Uh, back at
11    the store? I told her I didn't have enough money after the
12    drink and the chips and the comic book and lamp and salt
13    and pepper shakers, so I had to put a few things back. I also
14    told her, and this was probably a big mistake, that she
15    should've been more careful when calculating how much
16    money to give me. I was grounded for the rest of the week.

17        My parents have tried to give me an allowance; tried to
18    teach me to save half and spend the other. Somehow, I
19    always end up spending the saved half, the spending half,
20    and half of next week's allowance too. It's just useless. I'm
21    never gonna have any money.

22    *(Looks down at coins in hand.)* **Oops! I counted wrong.**
23    **Hey, can I borrow a nickel? I'll be sure to pay you back…**
24    **someday.**
25
26
27
28
29
30
31
32
33
34
35

# Momma's Boy

1     I think my mom's the most extra special person in the
2  whole wide world. It sounds weird to hear a guy talk about his
3  mom the way most guys talk about their girlfriends, right?
4  Nope, in the big picture, Mom's the only girl for me.
5     Who else but Mom is gonna run out to buy ingredients at
6  ten-thirty p.m. when the annual bake sale starts at eight a.m.?
7  Who else is gonna still love me even after I've smashed her
8  favorite vase while playing tackle football in the house? Who
9  else would dare to sit by me while I'm puking my guts out with
10  the flu. My girlfriend would have told me to hit the road a long
11  time ago, but not Mom. Mom's with you until the end.
12     I can talk to my mom about anything. Anything, you ask?
13  Uh-huh, even sex. She gives me straight answers and not a lot
14  of that you're-not-old-enough parent crap. Some of my friends
15  like to come talk to my mom instead of their own mothers
16  because mine is so cool. She doesn't get flustered when you tell
17  her something bad or off-the-wall. She listens calmly and then
18  says, "I see." After that, she'll tell you what she's been think-
19  ing while you've been spilling the beans. I may not always like
20  her answers, but hey, I don't always like what my girlfriend
21  tells me either and I still go out with her. "No" is hard to hear
22  from anyone.
23     The only problem I have with my mom is my dad. What a
24  jerk! Sometimes I can't figure out why she's married to him.
25  For starters, he's not my real dad, but he acts like it. I can't
26  even remember my real dad. I think his name is Larry. So, this
27  guy is really my stepdad, but since my real dad's been out of
28  the picture for so long, he makes me call him Dad. I'm not
29  gonna repeat what I call him in private. Let's just say it's a
30  body part and it doesn't see much sun.

1      Dad's always saying that I take advantage of my mom
2   and then hollering at me for something stupid. Like the
3   other day, I accidentally left the gate unlocked and my dog
4   got out. He ran around the neighborhood until somebody
5   called the animal catcher. He ended up at the pound. For-
6   tunately, he had his collar on so they called my mom to
7   come get him. It cost her fifty bucks to bail him out. Dad
8   freaked and said it would have to come out of my allowance.
9   At this rate, I'll probably be old enough for a job first before
10  I start getting my allowance again. But it's that kind of thing
11  that bugs me about Dad. It's not like I did it on purpose.
12      Whenever I make a wish, I wish for him to go very far,
13  far away. The only thing wrong with this is that Mom would
14  probably go with him and then where would I be? Mom
15  tells me to go easy on Dad, that he's just worried about me
16  'cause he knows how boys my age are and that he really
17  loves me. Yeah, right! If he really loved me he'd let me have
18  my allowance back instead of making me pay back every
19  penny. He really needs to take a lesson from Mom. She
20  slipped me a fifty and a kiss the other day! Isn't she the best?
21
22
23
24
25
26
27
28
29
30
31
32
33
34
35

# Daddy's Little Girl

1    There's no one more wonderful than my dad. A lot of other
2 girls think their boyfriends are so great or that some movie
3 star is just to die for. As far as I'm concerned, they all get sec-
4 ond place next to my dad.

5    My dad is really kind and generous. He's always slipping
6 me a twenty before I go to the mall. He lets me keep the change
7 from errands too. He'll say, "Keep the change!" no matter
8 how much it is. Sometimes, he'll even give me a tip.

9    Dad does other crazy, nutty stuff, too. When it's time for
10 dinner, he'll order a pizza or treat us to BK Lounge instead of
11 making us eat something healthy. He says it's got to be healthy
12 enough or else the government wouldn't let the restaurants
13 serve it. All my friends like to come over to my dad's 'cause
14 he'll take us wherever we want to go. It doesn't matter if it's
15 the movies, the skating rink, or miniature golf, Dad's always
16 game. Once Dad even took us on The Titanic. It's this giant
17 old-fashioned wooden roller coaster. It's really scary but Dad
18 said that life was too short not to go on fast, scary roller coast-
19 ers. Dad even gets up early to watch Saturday morning
20 cartoons. Is that cool or what?

21    Next to Dad, Mom is so old and boring. She constantly
22 makes this really gross, nutritional stuff for dinner. She has all
23 these rules for stuff we're not allowed to do. Like I can't watch
24 R-rated movies or stay up past nine o'clock. She treats me like
25 a baby. Do you know anyone in middle school who has to go to
26 bed during prime time TV? I didn't think so. Mom never lets
27 me have any friends over if it's a school night, and I can never
28 talk to my boyfriend if Mom's around. She doesn't think I'm
29 old enough for a boyfriend. When I tell her Dad thinks I'm old
30 enough, she just rolls her eyes and says, "Oh, your father

1     thinks so..." She's just jealous that I'd rather spend time
2     with Dad. If it wasn't for that stupid judge, I'd be living
3     with Dad and having a blast all the time.
4        See, Mom and Dad got a divorce two years ago. They
5     share me and my brother, but we only get to see Dad on
6     scheduled days. Mom says that Dad tries really hard to
7     show her up and see that we have a good time with him so
8     that she'll look like the bad guy. Heck, he doesn't even have
9     to try! She goes out of her way to act like the bad guy! When
10    I tell her she could learn a lesson or two from Dad, she just
11    says that "Oh, your Father" line. Then again, she could try
12    as hard as she could, take me to the moon and back, but
13    she'd never be as cool as my dad. I guess I'll always be my
14    daddy's little girl.
15
16
17
18
19
20
21
22
23
24
25
26
27
28
29
30
31
32
33
34
35

# About the Author

Heather Henderson caught the theater bug at an early age but never got to say a line on-stage until she was a senior in high school. She performed in many ballets (where you're not allowed to talk) and then, in her first high school production, was cast as a deaf/mute character! It was not until *West Side Story* that she was able to utter the very memorable line, "Ooh, oobley, ooh" as Riff's girlfriend, Velma.

After high school, Heather attended Florida State University (and again, she didn't get to say any lines in *The Merry Widow*) where she decided to become a teacher. Teachers get to say lots of lines! Following graduation, Heather taught drama for four years at Galaxy Middle School in Deltona, Florida, teaching students to say all the lines she was never able to. She currently teaches seventh grade Language Arts at Galaxy.

Heather and her husband, Michael Green, and their five very dramatic cats are expecting the arrival of their own little thespian sometime in June. This is her first published book (but she has lots of others at home in a closet...).

# Order Form

Meriwether Publishing Ltd.
P.O. Box 7710
Colorado Springs, CO 80933
Telephone: (719) 594-4422
Website: www.meriwetherpublishing.com

*Please send me the following books:*

_____ **The Flip Side  #BK-B221**                                    **$14.95**
by Heather H. Henderson
*64 point-of-view monologs for teens*

_____ **Acting Natural  #BK-B133**                                   **$14.95**
by Peg Kehret
*Honest-to-life monologs, dialogs and playlets for teens*

_____ **Winning Monologs for Young Actors**      **$14.95**
**#BK-B127**
by Peg Kehret
*Honest-to-life monologs for young actors*

_____ **Encore! More Winning Monologs for**       **$14.95**
**Young Actors  #BK-B144**
by Peg Kehret
*More honest-to-life monologs for young actors*

_____ **Spotlight  #BK-B176**                                        **$14.95**
by Stephanie S. Fairbanks
*Solo scenes for student actors*

_____ **Get in the Act!  #BK-B104**                                  **$14.95**
by Shirley Ullom
*Monologs, dialogs and skits for teens*

_____ **Theatre Games for Young Performers  #BK-B188   $16.95**
by Maria C. Novelly
*Improvisations and exercises for developing acting skills*

These and other fine Meriwether Publishing books are available at your local bookstore or direct from the publisher. Use the handy order form on this page.

Name: _____

Organization name: _____

Address: _____

City: _____ State: _____

Zip: _____ Phone: _____

❑  **Check enclosed**

❑  **Visa or MasterCard #** _____

*Signature:* _____     Expiration date: _____

*(required for Visa/MasterCard orders)*

**Colorado residents:** Please add 3% sales tax.
**Shipping:** Include $2.75 for the first book and 50¢ for each additional book ordered.

❑  *Please send me a copy of your complete catalog of books and plays.*

# Order Form

**Meriwether Publishing Ltd.**
P.O. Box 7710
Colorado Springs, CO 80933
Telephone: (719) 594-4422
Website: www.meriwetherpublishing.com

*Please send me the following books:*

_____ **The Flip Side  #BK-B221**                          $14.95
by Heather H. Henderson
*64 point-of-view monologs for teens*

_____ **Acting Natural  #BK-B133**                         $14.95
by Peg Kehret
*Honest-to-life monologs, dialogs and playlets for teens*

_____ **Winning Monologs for Young Actors**               $14.95
**#BK-B127**
by Peg Kehret
*Honest-to-life monologs for young actors*

_____ **Encore! More Winning Monologs for**               $14.95
**Young Actors  #BK-B144**
by Peg Kehret
*More honest-to-life monologs for young actors*

_____ **Spotlight  #BK-B176**                              $14.95
by Stephanie S. Fairbanks
*Solo scenes for student actors*

_____ **Get in the Act!  #BK-B104**                        $14.95
by Shirley Ullom
*Monologs, dialogs and skits for teens*

_____ **Theatre Games for Young Performers  #BK-B188**  $16.95
by Maria C. Novelly
*Improvisations and exercises for developing acting skills*

These and other fine Meriwether Publishing books are available at your local bookstore or direct from the publisher. Use the handy order form on this page.

Name: _____

Organization name: _____

Address: _____

City: _____ State: _____

Zip: _____ Phone: _____

❏  Check enclosed

❏  Visa or MasterCard # _____

Signature: _____  Expiration date: _____

(required for Visa/MasterCard orders)

**Colorado residents:** Please add 3% sales tax.
**Shipping:** Include $2.75 for the first book and 50¢ for each additional book ordered.

❏  *Please send me a copy of your complete catalog of books and plays.*